The Man in the Window

The Man in the Window

- Creating a Cultural Shift in Modern Day Evangelism

David J. Howell

For more info: www.davidjhowell.com

Dedication

Stacy. Thank you. You are my best friend. We started this journey over twenty years ago. You have always been my biggest supporter, when I felt like nothing else made sense, and I was merely existing. I Love You.

To Emma Grace, Warnock, Katie, Ezra, Birdee Jayne, & Charlotte, if there is one thing that being your father has taught me, it is the countless ways that God has shown me his unconditional love through being your father. God continually reveals portions of his heart for all mankind, through my relationship with each of you.

Mom, you loved me and never left me. I love you, I love your redemption story. Steve, I've seen the father's heart through your love for me.

Lastly to my friend and mentor Wayne, thank you for saying yes to me. You made a promise 30 years ago to a scared young man, and we are still walking in it today. 'Preciate Ya!

THE MAN IN THE WINDOW

Creating a Cultural Shift in
Modern Day Evangelism

David J. Howell

FOREWORD

David Howell has proven himself as a man faithful to his family, church, his leaders and most importantly God. This book Man in the Window is not just a good story that will inspire you, but it is a revelation from the Holy Spirit that has been seen and lived through David's life.

Eutychus sat one evening listening to the Apostle Paul share about the revelation he had received from Jesus. We can't even imagine what he experienced just being in the presence of the man who would write two thirds of the New Testament. The room that night was crowded with people hungry to hear what Paul had to say. Because of the close quarters Eutychus decided to sit in the window of a three story building. Paul was leaving the next day so he felt the urgency to pour into his disciples as much as he could. One hour went into two and then into three and on and on. Midnight came and Eutychus had hung on as long as he could. Fast asleep he falls from the window to his death.

The Man in the Window reveals the current condition of the church age we are living in. Many believers began with the excitement of Eutychus but in their journey have begun to move in and out of sleep. The drowsiness has turned into a pull from the world into an attitude of abandonment of the faith. Now here we are not even remembering the wonderful encounters of the Holy Spirit and the miracles God did in our lives. We have forgotten the joy of our salvation.

David does an excellent job in walking you through the process of the deception of the roaring lion Satan, who seeks whom he may devour. David exposes his tactics and then gives the principles of living in the Spirit and overcoming in your journey. This book teaches us how to connect as the church together in the Spirit of Christ and win the lost and hurting in our city. I love this statement in the book:

A Church that is about "WE and Not ME," will begin to transform how we see not only our Sunday Services, but how we approach restaurants, cellphone stores, society, flights, schools, our workplaces. All these places are filled with individuals that are either in the window, or have already fallen out. They all need to hear an on-time word, from an on-time Father, that loves them unconditionally, right where they are at.

The Man in the Window does not leave you in the condition of being asleep but ends with the revelation of resurrection. Let's look at the end of the story. Eutychus was raised from the dead. That is where God wants to meet all of us. Any area of your life that needs a touch of the resurrection power of God, now is your time. This book will help you take a look at your life and move you into a new refreshing and communion with your Father God.

I pray your heart is touched, restored and refreshed while reading The Man in the Window. Mine truly was!

Pastor Terry Nance
Impact Church, Sherwood Ar.
Author: God's Armorbearer

David Howell's "The Man In The Window" is not just a clever take on a few verses in the Bible, although it is that. This book comes as revelation from within a deep place in David's experience.

It has been my pleasure to walk with David as his pastor and friend for most of his life. I can tell you that he lives what he talks about. I believe this book will bring timely answers to questions about the church moving forward in these uncertain days of cultural and generational transitions.

If you are looking for a significant book giving a timely focus for the church, this is one you should get.

E. Wayne Drain, Founding Pastor
City Church (formerly Fellowship of Christians)

INTRODUCTION

In everything that we do, we encounter a journey along the way. This passage and what it has spoken to me over the years, has been a spiritual journey that I wanted to share with you. The amazing thing about the scriptures is they are a living document, from a living God. The inspiration that has come from them and the way that particular scriptures can mean so many different things and inspire multiple thoughts and feelings is what I have come to love as I have studied the word.

The Bible is filled with stories, encounters, individuals, that all work to do one thing, and that is to ultimately communicate God's love for his people. Through the authors, we are able to follow some people on their life journeys over the years, like Moses, King David, Paul, and Peter. Others individuals we meet very briefly, whether it is only a record of their simple prayer such as Jabez, or if it is only an encounter with Christ such as the woman at the well. All of the individuals are what make up this wonderful love story. All throughout scripture, from beginning to end, it is constantly pointing us the reader towards a relationship with God.

In the book of Acts the twentieth chapter, we are introduced, albeit very briefly to an individual named Eutychus, we don't really know anything about him other than what is recorded in the following five verses of the chapter. This passage in particular is one that speaks to me as an individual, it speaks to our modern-day church, and it is one, that I believe speaks to modern day evangelism. It also on a more tragic level is representative of our broken society, and how we as the modern-day church fail to recognize the countless people that have had the same fate as our dear friend Eutychus.

We've all seen the story of Eutychus, played out in congregations throughout the world for thousands of years. This story has always been the passage, about focus, don't be like the young man that went to the house church meeting and at some point lost his focus, and fell three stories to his death. In a way you have a young man, first pull away from the congregation, then you have him lose focus as he begins to drift into a deep sleep. Eventually falling, in a sense, away from the congregation to his death.

I remember this passage always being a warning, if you leave the church and lose your focus, you could fall asleep and eventually this error would leave you alone, separated from the church and spiritually dead. As a youth pastor, I can remember sharing this message and it would be centered around encouraging the youth group to keep their focus, to stay involved, to live life to the fullest in their spiritual journey, even when things got uncomfortable. I would end the message encouraging the kids to explore their lives and see where they had moved from the center of the room to the edge, what part of their life were they struggling with to remain strong in their walk with the Lord.

If you have been involved in a church for any amount of time, we have all seen this familiar story take place, I'm sure in your own walk you have numerous times had someone you were close to, involved in church, perhaps even a spiritual leader, that for one reason or another eventually chose to walk away from the church. For me, this played out at a very young age, in my home town of Russellville, AR. I can remember sitting in the congregation and watching my father speak at the front, praying for people, he was a fiery man, with a compassionate and generous heart.

It is my hope and prayer that as you read this, you will be blessed. I pray that you will be encouraged, the Holy Spirit will speak to you as you turn through these pages, and read the testimonies and what I feel God has laid on my heart for the modern-day church in today's world. We are not called to be individuals that merely sit on the sideline, but there is a battle out there in our world, and it is fought daily. The outcome has already been written, with the blood of the Cross. It's the Journey in between, that determines whether or not we were successful.

"It's a dangerous business, Frodo, going out your door. You step onto the road, and if you don't keep your feet, there's no knowing where you might be swept off to." — **J.R.R. Tolkien, <u>The Lord of the Rings</u>**

The Story of Eutychus -

On the first day of the week we came together to break bread. Paul spoke to the people and, because he intended to leave the next day, kept on talking until midnight. There were many lamps in the upstairs room where we were meeting. Seated in a window was a young man named Eutychus, who was sinking into a deep sleep as Paul talked on and on. When he was sound asleep, he fell to the ground from the third story and was picked up dead. Paul went down, threw himself on the young man and put his arms around him. "Don't be alarmed," he said. "He's alive!" Then he went upstairs again and broke bread and ate. After talking until daylight, he left. The people took the young man home alive and were greatly comforted.

Acts 20:7-12

1 | Gravity Always Pulls

When I picture a window, there is always something that draws me to the outside. Perhaps it was the lure of fresh air or a cool breeze. For some people, it's the temptation that lures them away from the inner circle, but shame that keeps them from re-entering. I've always found it easier to move away from something, but harder to move back.

I'm sure if you have ever been to a playground you have experienced the merry-go-round. My kids love to pile onto that toy at the playground and sit or lay in the middle. When we start pushing it, they will laugh, with cries for me to go faster. In the beginning, all the children will start in the center, where there is very little pressure from outside forces drawing them to the edge.

As the speed intensifies on the merry-go-round, there is a slight pull for them to re-position closer to the edge. The children move from the center towards the edge, where they feel, an even greater pull, attracting them to the edge of the merry-go-round. Eventually, they will end up on the very edge, hanging off, where the force is not linear, it is exponential. As the children move from the center, the force draws them faster and harder, until they can no longer hang on, ending with them falling off the merry-go around. The only way to stop the force drawing the children from the center, to the middle, to the outside and eventually propelling them off the merry-go-round, is the outside force of me their father, slowing the event, to where it stops spinning, and they can re-position themselves.

I would venture to say, the gravitational pull on the church today is not linear. It is exponentially growing as people are drawn to the outer windows of the church today. There is always something that entices them to that next step. Shame, unforgiveness, unbelief, addictions, and temptations are exponential forces, that make it impossible for them to turn around at any point and move away from the window and back into the center of the room. Just like with the merry-go-round, the only way for them to overcome any of their barriers to move from the outside back into the inside of the room, is an outside force, their heavenly father. The presence of God offers restoration, forgiveness, faith, deliverance from addictions, and victory over temptations.

If you have been involved in a church for any amount of time, then you are unfortunately all too familiar with this scenario. I'm sure in your own walk you had numerous times when someone you were close to, for one reason or another chose to walk away from the church. Perhaps it was a friend, a spouse, a sibling, or even a parent. Maybe it was someone in church leadership, the pastor, or worship leader. For me, this played out at a very young age, in my hometown of Russellville, Arkansas. I can remember sitting in the congregation and watching my father speak at the front and praying for people. He was a fiery man with a compassionate and generous heart.

"MY FATHER THE EVANGELIST"

My father had come to know the Lord in what is known as the "Jesus Movement" of the 1970's. This of course was decades before the invention of modern technology and the internet. Information did not travel as it does today through Facebook statuses, Instagram Feeds, and Tweets. Some believe that this movement started on the West Coast, in a small church Calvary Chapel led by Pastor Chuck Smith. This congregation of

25, quickly grew to 500 being baptized weekly, and this church was eventually built. It housed over 2000 congregants that still operates today. There was no social media and there was not any instant access, as this move of God travelled with hippies, hitchhikers, and through music. There was Jesus Festivals throughout the US. It took a couple of years to reach South Arkansas, where my father was a Senior in a small town in the rural Arkansas Delta named McGehee.

My dad, would dedicate his life to the Lord, in 1972, and his whole school was on fire for this new thing called Jesus. There were revivals breaking out throughout the Midwest and south, as it had continued to spread from the West Coast. My father would end up leaving after his high school graduation, and travelling with another young man, who was involved in the Jesus Movement at a small Arkansas College named Arkansas Tech University, in Russellville. They travelled that year, hitchhiking when they didn't have the funds for gas, but they travelled all over the Midwest sharing the gospel, leading meetings, and spreading the Gospel everywhere that would have them. They slept in people's living room floors. It was a time of rapid evangelism and growth.

My Father, would end up coming back to McGehee after a year on the road, and was truly a transformed man on a mission from God. His parents didn't understand what was happening to their son, nor what he had been doing for the year away. He agreed at their wish, to enter college, which is where he met my mother, and they were soon married. He led my mom to the Lord, not long after they met in the lunchroom of Henderson State University. He would lead bible studies at the college, and their group would get together with other movements from around the state travelling and having church together whenever they could. My mother and father eventually dropped out of college, and moved back to his hometown, where he worked with a local church as their youth pastor. A man of the word, he would memorize chapters of the bible. He taught himself to read Greek, so that he could understand the original language, but at this same time there was a different side to him and his life.

3

My father was moving from the center of the room, to the edge. He had begun drinking again. There was an extra-marital affair, and he was sliding into the window not living the life internally that he was displaying for people on the outside. My mom reached out to some of their friends that my father was accountable to, and they made a decision that they would move from the small town of McGhee to the town of Russellville, where the Jesus Movement had been so prevalent.

Fellowship of Christians was a group of hippies that loved Jesus, and this group was birthed on the campus of Arkansas Tech University. When they all looked up after graduation, they decided they didn't want to quit meeting just yet. They didn't fit in anywhere. They had crazy worship music, they saw miracles happening everywhere, and their university had been flipped upside down by the Jesus Movement of the 1970's. When my father and mother arrived it was 1978, the church had three elders all under the age of 25.

This is the church I would be born into. I was baptized in this church by my father, and the Senior Pastor Wayne Drain. I would see my father involved on Sundays, praying for people, and continuing to travel and share the gospel. However, as I became older, he once again began to move from the center of the room to the edge. My parents would fight, they would argue, and eventually the man I saw at home was not the same person the congregation would see on Sundays. My dad would eventually quit going to church with us. My mom would carry me and my three sisters to church each week. Dad said if we would change churches, he would go with us. That never happened. He had walked away from a relationship with God. When I was nine, my dad had another affair, and my mother left him. She moved all of us to her hometown of Magnolia, so that she could go back to college, and my amazing grandparents could help her go to school and raise us. Dad would never go back to church, living a life of alcoholism, and continued failed relationships.

For me, at the age of nine, the only explanation ever given to me about my father's absence was the often quoted, but misquoted verse "Pride comes before the fall." That was the best description that the church leaders could give me, for why my dad, who I knew loved the Lord, would walk away from his marriage and family. There were signs all over the room. He didn't just one day quit serving the Lord.

My Father, had done just as Eutychus did. He had set out with great intentions, but through the course of his journey when things became uncomfortable, he had moved to a new location, spiritually in a sense, that was more comfortable. Eventually, finding his way to a window, and falling completely away from the congregation and the church, more importantly away from a relationship with the Lord. In fifteen short years, my father, who had experienced love, forgiveness, grace, redemption, was laying in the street, alone, ashamed, broken, and away from God.

"WE ALL KNOW THAT SOMEONE"

Now there isn't anything unique about my story, and sadly about the testimony of my Father. This is a story that we all have experienced. We all know that someone, who was on fire for the Lord, and one day chose to walk away.

Not everyone leaves the congregation for the same reasons, as my Father did. I've met people that were offended by the church. Unfortunately, this is all too common. Perhaps they experienced hurt, manipulation, or offense by someone who was a leader of the church. Maybe there was a time when they needed help, counseling, a friend, and no one from the congregation stepped up to assist them in the way they felt was needed.

"WHAT IF?"

As I mentioned earlier, this passage was a go to one for me to preach. That the tables were on the young man who lost his focus, became uncomfortable, and moved to a more comfortable place in the room. This passage, in a weird way, was always about my father. I could see my father as Eutychus moving from the room, to the edge, and eventually falling out.

This passage was one that invoked fear. If you fall asleep at church, then you could die. Now I'm not sure that any pastor has ever actually preached that, but I honestly wouldn't be surprised. What if the focus on this passage wasn't about the young man, but about everyone else in the room that failed to recognize the young man moving from the center of the room, to the edge?

What if the true message here was taking the burden off the young man? Inside the church, the burden was always placed on the young man who was tired and uncomfortable. What if the burden of this passage shifted to the rest of the people that failed to recognize what was happening when there was a shift in this young man's posture and location, to where he was headed was not a safe place?

For this to happen, then the Gospel is not based in fear. The most quoted scripture in the bible is "For God so Loved the world, that he gave his only son, so that whosoever believes in him, shall not perish, but have ever lasting life." This isn't a Gospel of Fear, it is a Gospel of Love.

For this to happen, then our Church has to shift from an inward focus to an outward focus.

2 | WHEN LIFE GETS UNCOMFORTABLE

If there is one thing that I've learned about growing up in the Bible Belt, everyone seems to know Jesus. Everyone has had an encounter with church, not always Jesus, but definitely the church. There is an elder in our home church with a burning desire to share the Gospel. We like to joke that he has probably knocked on every door in our city at least twice to share the Gospel. Dr. Travis is a retired professor, from Arkansas Tech University. He was on the campus, during the Jesus Movement of the 1970's, and actually had several of these "Jesus freaks" in his classes over the years. He now serves as an elder, of our local church, City Church. Formerly known as Fellowship of Christians that started on the campus of Arkansas Tech University in 1972. Dr. Travis, was a member of another congregation in town until the early 2000's when he felt led to come and join what was happening at City Church.

One thing that he has carried with him over the years, is the desire to share the Gospel with everyone that he meets. A wonderful teaching pastor and gatherer, he has led a group of men that meet in his garage every Wednesday morning at 6 in the morning to gather, study the word, and pray for the city and state. This meeting of men, has been meeting every week for over 35 years. It's always encouraging, when I am able to attend the gatherings. There are men sitting amongst each other, ranging in age from 25 – to young men in their 70's. These men share a passion for an encounter with God, hunger for more knowledge, and a strong prayer walk.

A couple of years ago, Dr. Travis asked me to commit to going out with him once a week to learn how to pray with people and share the gospel. I must admit I wasn't sure what this would look like, but I was on Pastoral Staff. I felt like there had to be a better way to tell people about the Lord then simply waiting on them to show up in our church.

Dr. Travis, would pick me up each night, and we would to go to the laundromats in our town. If you have ever been an outdoorsman, you know what the term "honey hole" means. If you fish, it's the one place in the lake where you know when your cork hits the water, you almost certainly will come back with a fish on the other end. For Dr. Travis, the laundromats were his "honey holes."

When you think about it, sharing the Gospel in a laundromat is an awesome opportunity. You have a captive audience and people can't run from you, because they can't leave their laundry. Sometimes it seemed odd, to walk in and immediately introduce yourself to a complete stranger. At times it could feel awkward as people were folding their clothes in front of you. I bet that I have seen 20 different ways to fold towels! But I was pleasantly surprised at the positive response we received. Dr. Travis had a spiritual questionnaire that he had spent years perfecting. We would ask questions and give an opportunity to talk to us about their own spiritual journey. We would then pray with them, and we saw many people give their hearts to the Lord.

I can remember one day, when we were the only two in the laundromat that spoke English as a primary language. Myself, having four semesters of Spanish, knew only enough to say "Como se dice en espanol" translated to "How do you say this in Spanish". Dr. Travis happened to have a biblical track on salvation printed in Spanish in his folder, so we pulled it out. There were two young men washing their clothes who were very open to visiting with us as I read the literature in my broken Spanish. The first young man would end up praying a prayer of salvation, then turning to his friend and leading him to the Lord as we watched in amazement. It was a great day as we watched these two young men make the commitment to serve Jesus.

Living in the Bible Belt, everyone seems to know Jesus. What I wasn't prepared for was the overwhelming number of people that we encountered that knew Jesus, yet chose not to live for him or be in church. As we would visit with people and pray with them, most had at one time or another been in church, but were offended and quit going. It never failed, every night, every person we met, was similar to Eutychus in so many ways. Maybe they were in church when they were growing up, perhaps they left church when they got divorced or went with a grandparent while growing up. Some people were still involved in church, but you could see the hurt in their eyes. We would always get the opportunity to pray with people, and saw some pretty cool miracles over the course of time.

I can remember one afternoon, we encountered two college students, who were of another religion. They did not believe in God. We shared with them, and they allowed us to pray for them. One young man, even prayed that if God was real, he would reveal himself to him. I received what I felt was a Word of Knowledge for this young man as he prayed. I felt like the Holy Spirit spoke to me, and said that later that day, the young man would receive a gift, something free that he wasn't expecting. It wasn't a large object, but it would be a nice gesture and he would have joy in receiving it. I felt like this would be the young man's confirmation that the God he had just prayed to was real. I shared what I felt like the Lord

9

showed me. I then gave my phone number to the young man, and asked him to call me when he received the gift.

A couple of hours later, I received a call from the excited young man. As he walking across campus, a friend walked up with an extra Frappuccino coffee from Mcdonalds. They had given the young man a free one and he didn't have any need for it, so he gave it to the young man that we had just prayed for. This young man, was in shock, and surprised that the God he had prayed to was so big, yet at the same time concerned with something as little as a $4 drink from McDonald's as a gift to him.

"ONE RAINY NIGHT"

One rainy night, Dr. Travis picked me up to go to our usual fishing spots or honey hole as we said in Arkansas terms. Neither one of us thought anyone would be crazy enough to be out doing laundry in the down pour we were experiencing. We could barely see out of the windows of the vehicle as we drove through town. Both of us made excuses for why no one would be out in this. As we pulled into the first laundromat, we noticed an older couple in their 70's. The wife was doing the laundry and the husband was leaning against the machines.

Dr. Travis took the lead as we introduced ourselves. We asked questions and they answered. Turns out the wife was in church, twice a week, and I'm sure she served on every committee they had. They lived out in the country and attended a small church close to their home. However, her husband, we will call him 'John,' was pretty quiet. He acknowledged that he knew Jesus, but refused to go to church.

One area that people who attend church miss is spending time with people that do not have a personal relationship with God. This is when we believe that someone attending church will be the solution to all of their problems. I have conversations all the time, with people sharing about their children, spouse, a loved one, that does not have a personal relationship with God, and most times it ends with the statement 'If I could just get them to church'. Well that's not the solution.

It is part of the solution. The writer of Hebrews in Chapter 10:25 writes "not forsaking the assembling of ourselves together, as *is* the manner of some, but exhorting *one another,* and so much the more as you see the Day approaching." As believers, we should want to be together to encourage one another, to pray together, to submit to those that feel called to share with us the Gospel message. The church gathering is one piece of the puzzle, but it's not every piece.

As we began to visit with John, we learned that he was in church as a young man, nearly 45 years before. But something very serious had happened and he had been deeply hurt by someone in the ministry. As a young man, he had walked away from all religion, and more importantly a relationship with Christ. He was offended, and I completely understand why. He had done the honorable thing, and stayed with his wife, but over time it got easier and easier to just allow her to go to church, and him stay away. 'John' had started out in the middle of the room, but over time moved to the window. There was an offense, and he was hurt by the church. He had moved to the window, just as Eutychus had, in an effort to deal with the pain. Surely over the last 45 years, someone in the room, had to of noticed that this devout lady was showing up to every service, without her husband she had been married to for over 50 years.

We asked John if he would like to make a decision to start following Christ, and he said while he knew he should, it was too late. 'John' was carrying 45 years of hurt, unforgiveness, and pain around with him. I watched as his wife teared up, knowing what her husband was carrying around. So, we asked 'John' if we could at least pray for him before we left. He reluctantly agreed. Even if someone doesn't accept Christ as their Lord and Savior doesn't change the fact that we are still sent to *Love our Neighbors*. Why wouldn't we offer to *pray for this man,* and *Love him exactly where he was*.

As Dr. Travis started praying for him, I felt the Holy Spirit tell me to pray for his lower back, on the right side, where he had a disc issue. This happens fairly often, when we recognize that God does still speak to us. It

11

is always amazing at what the Holy Spirit can do. In spite of our efforts, God doesn't need me to heal this man, but he did want me to be obedient and step out in my own faith walk. My first reaction when I felt like I heard the Holy Spirit was to pray and ask God if this was my own thoughts, or was it from him. The next step was a step of Faith. Faith that what I had heard from the Holy Spirit was really from him.

When it was my chance to pray for 'John' I looked at him, and shared what I thought the Holy Spirit had revealed to me. Now when it comes to praying for people and the Lord speaking to us, let me be the first to say, it doesn't have to be awkward. I didn't look at 'John' and say "Thus sayeth the Lord, thou have an issue with thy back." We sometimes miss it, when we hear what we think the Lord is telling us. I simply explained, that I believe the Lord does still speak to us, and that I felt like the Lord had highlighted his lower back to me and if it was, then I would love to pray for it. He looked down at me and shook his head "NO." About that time his wife yelled "'John'! You know exactly what he's talking about, most mornings you struggle to even get out of bed!" Had it been my wife, I would have been scared.

I looked back at John and he slowly nodded yes, almost embarrassed that he hadn't admitted it. I was excited to see the Holy Spirit at work in this man's life. Encouraged that I had heard the Holy Spirit speak to me for this man, I explained to John that God knew who he was, and wanted to heal his back. Then asked if he would let me pray for his back. Dr. Travis and I laid hands on his lower back and began praying and we could feel the spot begin to get hot. When we asked 'John' if he could physically feel anything in his back. He acknowledged that it was heating up. As we finished, we could see John begin to tear up. When we asked how his back felt, his back had been healed. At this point Dr. Travis asked him a second time if he would like to ask Jesus into his heart, and begin living for him and he agreed.

There is nothing more beautiful than seeing someone who has been living away from God, come back. Here was a man, much like Eutychus who had moved away from God, eventually falling away. 'John' had been gone for 45 years, yet in one instance and one encounter from God, he was fully alive again. I can't help but wonder how many more people in our world are just waiting on one encounter from God. One person to come to where they are and share the good news with them.

"RIGHT WHERE YOU ARE"

This man, had gone through much of his adult life with hurt from the church. He had made a decision to leave the church. His wife had remained. I believe we could have been at his wife's church for a year of revival meetings and he still wouldn't have graced the doors with his presence. What this man needed was not an encounter with the Church, but he needed an encounter with the Holy Spirit. Which is exactly what happened to him on that rainy night in the laundromat.

As Dr. Travis and I left that night, we were encouraged by the encounter with 'John'. We were excited at the new life that faced this couple after years of unforgiveness and pain. Now they had a new relationship. The one question we had as we drove away, was how many more people were there just like 'John'? How many more individuals were there, who had moved to the outer parts of the room like Eutychus, when it got uncomfortable? How many people had been offended or hurt by the local church, or church leadership, and chosen to sit in the window eventually falling away? We could have church every night in our building and never have an encounter like that night in the pouring rain.

The world is filled with people just like this gentleman, and a building with four walls just isn't the answer. It's a personal encounter with their heavenly father, with the Holy Spirit. If we are filled with the Holy Spirit, then we owe it to these people to meet them where they are at, and not just sit in our comfortable sanctuaries hoping they show up. At this point the message shifts from fear to Love.

3 | GOOD INTENTIONS

"On the first day of the week we came together to break bread. Paul spoke to the people and, because he intended to leave the next day, kept on talking until midnight" ACTS 20:7

I've tried to picture the setting some two thousand years ago, when Eutychus set out with his friends for that fateful evening with the Apostle Paul. I try to picture a young man full of excitement about what has been happening in his city. There were probably many stories of the great speaker that would be visiting that evening to teach on Christianity. Paul would have been well known and revered throughout the land. I don't believe that as Eutychus left his home that night, he looked his mother in the eyes and said "Hey mom, I'm going out with my friends to hear Paul speak tonight. We will probably be out all night, and at some point, I plan on falling out of the window and breaking my neck and will die. Don't worry though, I will see you in the morning." I have to think that this was the furthest thing from the young man's mind that night. He was simply going to a gathering to hear and learn about this amazing new message of Christ.

Archaeology would tell us that this wasn't a large room. It would have had lamps in it, open windows, and probably didn't have the modern comforts that we have in our services. There would be heat coming from the dimly lit lamps, because there was no modern air conditioning to control the environment. As the night went on, at some point, the young man became uncomfortable where he was. Perhaps he began in the center of the room, or even sitting on the front row. There was a point in the evening, where he was no longer comfortable and he moved to the window perhaps to get fresh air or perhaps he was dozing off, and thought that fresh air may help him stay awake.

I've been guilty of this when on a long car ride. I roll down the windows of the vehicle, just to get the rush of fresh air on my face. Turning the music up loud hardly ever works when you have a car full of sleeping kids and a wife. We have all tried, at some point or another, rolling the window down to wake you, when we become tired of driving on long trips. This may be what Eutychus was doing in moving to the window. Once in the window, you have a whole new view. The room has changed, not to mention, you can see everything down below you in the streets. This worldview was not available to you when you are sitting in the middle of the room.

"DON'T LOSE FOCUS"

This would be the part of the message where a Pastor would preach about how Eutychus had lost focus. He should have been paying more attention and it was his fault he wasn't standing in the midst of everyone. A good preacher would use this message and say that "if you lose focus, you could die." Life happens though. And I don't think anyone that I've known that has walked away from Christ set out to do that.

When my father decided to quit coming to church with us, at first it was just once, but then maybe it was hunting season, and it was easier for him to be at the deer camp for the weekend. I don't think that first Sunday he stayed home was because he was planning on leaving the church. Perhaps, he felt shame that he wasn't being the man of God that he had been in the past. It may have been uncomfortable to go to church, and have to put on a front for his friends. Regardless, what he deemed uncomfortable, it was easier for him to shift locations from the front of the room, to the back of the room.

I've had people confide in me, that there are times when they don't want to be in church. Not because they don't believe in God or not because they aren't walking with the Lord. They just would rather not have to make uncomfortable small talk with other individuals.

Life happens. There are countless opportunities where people for one reason or another move from where they started out in the center of the room to where it's just a little more comfortable. Jesus said in Luke 9:23, ***And he said to all, "If anyone would come after me, let him deny himself and take up his cross daily and follow me."*** Deny yourself, take up your torture instrument and follow me. It's not always comfortable to live a life following Jesus. But we have Faith, in the one that ultimately died for our sins.

I believe that being uncomfortable in church has two parts. The first phase is often brought on by the Church. We have cast this vision in modern times that we all have it together. My wife is a photographer, a very talented one at that. She has a very creative eye, and always seems to capture the best moments. Her social media is a history of the many adventures, moments, and events in our children's life. When she shares them on social media, everyone is amazed at the moment she has managed to capture. What people fail to realize is these moments that we capture and share for the world to see are the highlights of that moment. We aren't posting the kids fighting, their room destroyed, the mountain of laundry awaiting us, or the upset teenager not getting their way. We choose what access we want the outside world to have.

With the invention of Social Media, we are all living a life of comparison. Comparing our lives to the "moments" of those that we look up to. With this comparison, we often times bring on manufactured uncomfortableness to our congregations. We want the world and our friends to think that everything is always perfect. Others in the church, think that if their life isn't perfect, then they probably don't need to be in church.

"DAD FAILS"

One thing I appreciate from our Senior Leader Chris Abington, is that he is a father of 6 kids, just like myself. Chris and his wife Tara, are amazing parents, who love their kids, almost as much as they love the Lord. One thing that Chris has always been good with me about is that we are very transparent in our relationship, and aren't afraid to share what we call "Dad Fails." Let's face it, I have six kids, and that leaves a lot of room for me to have failures as a parent. I miss the mark pretty regularly, but one thing I appreciate with Chris, is that we are open and I can share these failures, and not feel judged. Chris may have some advice, and he will usually laugh with me, but then offer what he may or may not have experienced similar to that situation.

Having this outlet, allows me to share that life isn't perfect. My wife is great about sharing all the "moments." We can't expect others to believe that we don't have those other "fails" as well. So, we have to find a way for the world to know that life is messy. Being a Christian is messy, being a husband is messy, being a father is messy, and living life with others is definitely messy. We need others to share this with though. We can't get uncomfortable with our own "messy fails" and walk away from the best support system known to man!

"IT'S NOT ABOUT YOU"

There are dozens of ways for people to become offended in the church. When that happens, we become uncomfortable, and need to find an outlet to move to in order to escape the offense. Over the years, I've seen people leave the church because they didn't like the way the preacher delivered messages. I have offended people at sporting events when I didn't acknowledge them in a crowd full of fans, even though I never saw them.

We get offended when the preacher asks for tithes and offerings or perhaps it is the song choice of the worship leader. The lights are too bright, the lights are too low, the music is too loud, or it's too soft. Let's face it, in modern times there are thousands of ways for us to become offended or uncomfortable in the Modern Church.

When the focus of the church should be on a personal relationship with Christ, we've turned it into something about us. For me as a young man growing up, Christianity was just a long list of rules. Rules that I had to follow if I wanted to be loved. Don't have pre-marital sex, don't drink, don't cuss, don't look at pornography, don't do drugs, and don't have a sex-drive. I knew everything the church stood against, but very little about what it stood for.

My joy came in how well I had done the prior week upholding all the "laws" of what I thought it meant to be a Christian. I felt like my sin caused God to love me less, he would be angry with me. To me, growing up felt like God had a bunch of loud "No's". It wasn't until I had a personal relationship with him, that I began to hear his "Yes" he had over my life. God wasn't saying "No" to everything, in fact he was screaming "Yes" but within his protective boundaries. God never asks anything of us, or takes away things unless he is wanting to bless us with something else or protect us.

God is saying *Yes* to us. The enemy wants to trap us in this lie that we aren't good enough, we aren't pure enough; we aren't perfect enough. He wants us to see the church's perfect "moments" and feel like we don't belong, and we should be uncomfortable and move to the outside of the room, where we can feel a little less judged. When all we may need, is a friend that we can look at and say "Hey, let me tell you, how I missed the mark this week."

"YOUR FIRST 'MOMENT' AS A NEW BELIEVER"

In today's world, people come into the church with good intentions, to come into a relationship with Christ. This is their defining moment, whether it's being baptized on a Sunday morning, or coming down in front of the congregation to accept Jesus as their Lord and Savior. This is your first "moment".

What happens next is when it gets uncomfortable. When we begin as a church to show every thing we are against it is more comfortable to move to the side of the room. One of the first things the enemy will do is try to remind you of who you were. He doesn't want you in this place. He wants to point out all your mishaps and shame you for all your sins. This will allow you to feel uncomfortable, and then you begin to feel like maybe you don't belong on the front row.

When we disobey God, we are basically saying "I don't trust you." I know that you say you know the plans you have for me, but I don't trust that you really meant that for me. So we move to the part of the room where we don't have to be fully engaged. We are in the church, we have what we feel like is a comfortable enough relationship where we acknowledge we are there, but it's more comfortable in the window.

"IT'S ALL ABOUT ME"

In the window, I can simply be there at the service, but I don't have to deal with the extras. I can check it off my list. Others don't see me, but I see them. We simply slip into receive mode. We come to church each week to receive something, but rarely pour back in. It's easier, and no one can disappoint us when we aren't involved.

The dangerous thing about a receive mentality, is we have cheapened the purpose of church into a consumer mentality. If I'm only there to "take," I begin to think with the consumerism mindset. I become an expert on the Worship Music, too loud, too soft. The Pastor's messages – too long, too short, not enough scriptures, too many scriptures.

We look at our children's ministries differently. We see the nursery as a "Daycare" to simply drop our kids off for a couple of hours so they aren't climbing on us. When in fact, the church desperately needs us. It needs workers to pour into our children, worship leaders, volunteers, and a servant's heart!

A church with a consumerism mentality is destined to fail as the focus is shifted from what God is trying to do in our hearts, to what we can do to serve the congregation. I believe you can have leaders, worship leaders, and a children's ministry with perfect hearts. However, there is still a large part of the congregation with a consumerism mindset, that is only there to take and to check it off their list. These are the ones that I worry about. The first time they experience discomfort, then they will move to the side of the room where it's easier to sit.

I believe that like Eutychus didn't expect when he left his home that night to hear Paul, that he would eventually fall asleep, and tumble three stories to his death. Neither are the countless believers in our churches. Neither was my father, who walked solidly with the Lord for fifteen years, before moving to the Window, where it was more comfortable. Nobody sets out to fail.

4 | THE INVISIBLE MAN

"Seated in a window was a young man named Eutychus, who was sinking into a deep sleep as Paul talked on and on." ACTS 20:9

So now Eutychus has moved to the corner of the room, not where he set out to be, but for one reason or another where he is. He's tired, he's discouraged, and probably focused on other things than when he first arrived. Maybe's he's gazing out the window. Regardless, he is no longer where he was when the night began.

My father passed away in 2012. I can't tell you the number of stories that strangers have shared with me about ministry moments, testimonies, and miracles that they saw him involved with. For me, at the time, a young man in my mid-thirties, I struggled with this. My initial reaction was wanting to share with them my personal experiences. The man that they were talking about, was not the same man that I knew. The man that they knew and remembered was just like Eutychus sitting in the middle of the room. The guy I carried memories of was the man that later would move to the window, and fall three stories to his death.

We see in the church today, someone you may know that was at one point on fire for God. Now you may see them only every so often in your church. You used to be in bible study with them, maybe they came to your small group, but now they have too many other things happening to be able to make it. I can remember sitting in the balcony on Sunday nights, because my mom was in the choir. That's where she could see me and my sisters if we misbehaved. Dad was at home, perhaps watching Sunday night football. Maybe the spouse has a struggle with pornography, and he doesn't feel comfortable at church, so he stays home while the wife continues going to church.

Maybe this is you. Maybe you have been offended by the church like our friend John earlier. It's just easier for you to not have a personal relationship with the Lord, because of the time that you were wronged. I honestly can't tell you how many people I have met in the streets that no longer attend church because they have been offended by something.

"DID THAT REALLY JUST HAPPEN?"

For one reason or another, we all know someone unfortunately that is no longer in the room with us, but now are on the window sill. As I was reading this passage, my first reaction was how would you like to be the guy that had to interrupt the Apostle Paul? "Hey Pastor Paul, excuse me Pastor Paul, but I just saw someone fall out of that window over there." I've seen car wrecks, accidents, but I've never witnessed anyone fall out of a window before.

Then I became convicted. Did no one see this young man dozing off in the window? Surely someone noticed that Eutychus was no longer sitting in the middle of the room. Did he not have to walk by anyone to get to the window? Was everyone in the room so intrigued by what Paul was saying that he didn't recognize the young man move from the middle of the room to the window sill?

If my kids are in the yard playing, I keep a very watchful eye on them making sure that they don't go into the street. Not because the street is the best or most fun place to play and I don't want them to have any fun. I don't want them in the street, because it's a dangerous place where they can be hurt if they go into it. I don't wait until they walk out of the yard to remind them. I let them know when they are walking towards it. How did this young man, walk from the middle of the room, to the window, where it's a dangerous place and no one notice?

Today we live in a world so connected, where I know what you ate for breakfast, lunch, and dinner. I know what your kids are wearing for the first day of school. I can tell you what your family did for vacation. Mainly because I hit like on the button as I scrolled through Instagram or Facebook. Yet our society is full of people sitting in the window sill, or worse have fallen out like 'John' from the laundry mat, and we choose to ignore it.

When you stop and think about it, there is probably multiple individuals you can think of that started out with you, or have stood with you in the room. Yet for one reason or another they've gotten uncomfortable or offended and moved to the outer part of the room. We however, are guilty of choosing to ignore their absence. We instead like their daily Facebook posts, move on, and only discuss them when it's convenient. Maybe someone was in that small room and they saw Eutychus sitting in the window and falling asleep, but it wasn't convenient to get up and go across the room to him.

When it's a Consumer mindset, we are so overly concerned with what is happening in our own lives, that we fail to see the young married couple struggling financially, or the single mom with multiple kids. We are too focused on the how we are being fed by the church to look around and figure out who needs us in the congregation.

It is so much easier for us to be so focused on our own personal needs that we are no longer looking around to see what's happening around us. We've all had those conversations and we all know who is struggling, yet it's easier for us to stand back at a distance and observe with judgement, rather than interacting with Compassion.

"YOU ARE NOT INVISIBLE"

I can remember a young lady that was a part of the church. She was a worshipper, she always stood at the front of the congregation, and worship her heart out on Sunday Mornings. She always had her notebook and Bible, scribbling away feverishly with the same intensity that she would worship with.

She had a past, and was open about being delivered from a life of addiction. She was doing everything she could to walk in this relationship with God. One day, I walked into a restaurant with some family and friends, and ran into her. I noticed that I hadn't seen her at church in a while, and I had wondered how she was doing. When we tried to talk to her, she couldn't make eye contact, and was in a hurry to move about her day. She had moved from the center of the room to the window, and as a church and Pastor, I had somehow missed it.

A couple of weeks later, I was in the grocery store, and noticed her at the front of the checkout line, so I made an effort to make my way to her. Once again, no eye contact. She was displaying all the familiar signs of someone struggling with drug addiction. This broke my heart, so I stopped her in the middle of the grocery store, and just took the opportunity to speak life to her. She allowed me to pray for her, and began crying as I prayed for her in the middle of the store.

She was crying because she heard from God that day. She was not invisible; she was not out of the reach of Christ. Although she is not back in our congregation, I ran into her again several weeks later and she was clean. I could see that fire in her eyes, as she allowed me to pray for her again in the store. She told me all about the church she was plugged into, and I felt peace for her.

Most times what someone needs is just to be seen. No way can I believe that Eutychus was invisible and no one saw him dozing off, no one saw him walk from the middle to the edge of the room. All he needed was for someone to see him. That's all 'John' needed that night in the laundry mat was for someone to see him, and in an instant, you had 45 years of un-forgiveness and pain wiped away.

The Cross is for everyone. When Jesus died on the cross, it wasn't for only the people that show up to church each week. It wasn't only for the people associated with a certain denomination. When Jesus died on the cross, no one was invisible. Therefore, if we are to obey the great command "to go out into all the world and make disciples," then invisible cannot be in our vocabulary.

People are owed an encounter with the Holy Spirit, and all believers are carrying it. The enemy wants these people to feel lonely, abandoned, and invisible, just like Eutychus. Sometimes just a brief encounter with someone is all a person needs.

Recently, I was on a flight from Redding to LAX, on a smaller plane. It was one of those early morning flights, where everyone is quiet, and no one even gets up. The flight attendant was sitting at the front of the plane facing the passengers. I said a simple prayer, as often times I like to do. I asked God "what would you want this young lady to know today?" Who wouldn't like to get a message from God each day? I know I wish most days that someone would share this with me. We know it's going to be encouraging and it's going to be uplifting. I felt like I heard the Holy Spirit say, "tell her that she is a good daughter, her father loves her, and everything is going to be ok."

As I am leaving the flight, everyone is in a hurry to get off the plane. I take my time getting up and making my way off. The flight attendant is standing at the front of the plane thanking everyone for travelling with their airline. When I get to her, I looked at her and told her "ma'am, I am a guy that likes to pray, and I was just praying for you and I felt like God wanted me to tell you a couple of things." Her face suddenly shifted and she looked up at me, as I continued. "I felt like the Lord told me that you were a great daughter, your dad loves you, and everything is going to be ok." She immediately began crying, and thanking me. She then opens up that her father had passed away recently, and that her ex-husband was taking her to court to try and take her son away and lose custody. She felt all alone.

She then allowed me to pray for peace and protection for her. When we finished, she asked if she could just give me a hug. I'm not sure what the pilots thought as they were walking out of the plane to see their flight attendant crying and hugging a passenger. I didn't know what to think either, except that it was an amazing moment where one of God's children were no longer invisible. They knew they weren't alone in their journey. I've come to enjoy these encounters because there is nothing better than getting the opportunity to speak life into individuals, and see how the quickly the Joy of the Lord can fall on a situation.

Honestly, had I not prayed for this lady it would have been just another day of work for her, and another day of travel for me. What happens when the Body of Christ begins to carry the presence of God outside the four walls of our churches into our cities, states, and everyday lives?

When the Church begins to see everyone, then it is no longer about ME, but now it is about We!

5 | WE NOT ME

"All these with one accord were devoting themselves to prayer, together with the women and Mary the mother of Jesus, and his brothers" ACTS 1:14

At what point did the church become about Me, rather than we? One common theme that I hear from people all the time is the desire for the church to be the Church of Acts in today's society. If we were the church of Acts, revival would break out. This scripture in Acts says it very clearly, "they were all with one accord, devoting themselves to prayer." They lived life together, they prayed together, and they were in homes together. The church was about *We,* not Me.

In our local church, we use the phrase, "We, not Me." It's something that the leadership team have defined that if we were going to truly be a church for the city, then our walk with the Lord should be "We and not Me."

What better way for the enemy to attack the church, than to start within our services. When we make the services about "Me," then they are no longer to praise God, but to praise man. I've been guilty of this before. I'll raise my hands in worship, but only if they play the song I like. I don't really like this song, or I wish it was the other worship leader leading today. They always turn the lights down too low during worship, or it's too bright in here. I've actually heard both of those complaints on the same morning. The younger generations want it dark and loud, and older generations want it bright and quiet. One conversation I have actually had with people is "I'd invite my friends but they have this guy's preaching this week, and I really don't like his style." My kids don't really like the new Youth Pastor, because he doesn't play enough games at Youth Group. "Oh great, why are they letting the Youth Pastor preach this week, he doesn't have near the experience our regular pastor does." Why can't our worship team play songs from this decade?

You see, we have too often made our services about ME. Churches are competing to get the most streamline experience. They are competing with vacations, competitive sports, and a day off, chores. Nothing is wrong with any of these, I fully believe that when you attend the church it should be done with excellence. The lights should work right, the worship team should sound like this isn't the first time they looked at the music, and the pastor should have been in prayer all week preparing to share what God's laid on his heart.

When all we are doing on Sundays is looking at everything through the lens of "ME," we fail to see the widow sitting by herself in the pew. We miss the youth who just wants to be seen and not be invisible. We miss the single mom worried about whether or not she is going to have food on the table. We miss the wife sitting by herself with her kids checked into the kid's center. All people sitting in the window, that by us choosing to not acknowledge because we have made our Worship Experience about ME and not, WE.

If we are too focused on ME, then we don't see the young man struggling with pornography. We don't see the struggles with alcohol abuse, and we don't see the pre-marital sex and financial struggles. All of these linear forces, propel our society to the window, for what they believe will be relief from all the pain, troubles, and shame they feel in the first place.

I'm sure that 'John' at the laundromat, had people notice that he wasn't in church. In the beginning perhaps there were conversations, and people recognizing that he wasn't with his wife. I'm sure in the beginning someone asked, but over time it became easier to just not acknowledge that he had an obvious hurt or offense from the place he had previously worshipped. 'John' became invisible sitting in the window and eventually falling out, not to be noticed for 45 years. I am sure people prayed for him; I know his wife did. But over time, it becomes easier for a congregation focused on ourselves and our needs to no longer have those uncomfortable conversations.

How many people do we know are sitting on the edge of their relationship with God, and we choose to not have those conversations because that would be uncomfortable? When we choose to ignore these problems that we see inside our congregations, they still exist, and they don't just disappear. Eventually though, with enough shame, unforgiveness, and ignorance, the pull by the enemy to the window will be strong enough that they will eventually lead out the window. They continue to sit on the edge of the room, feeling shame, hurt, pain, eventually losing focus on who God is in their life, and focusing on their offenses. When our focus is on "ME," then I am no longer looking around the room at others. I'm simply looking at Me and my wants and needs.

We weren't meant to go through life alone. We were meant to live in unity, worship together, grow together, and encourage one another. I believe living a Christian Life is much easier when it's spent simply focused on loving one another, rather sitting in judgement over our neighbor. I heard a preacher say one time that, "Satan knows your sin, but does not know your name. Jesus knows our name, but does not know our sin."

"GOOD MORNING! WELCOME"

Often times we have pre-conceived notions about individuals. Even if you have never met them before, you have an opinion. I've been guilty of this before. When I was a new youth pastor in my church, I asked the Pastor what he would like me to do on Sunday mornings. I was new to the church, and did not know a lot of the people in the congregation. The Pastor told me to stand in the lobby and greet people, and meet everyone that came in until I knew everyone at the church by name. Pretty daunting task if you ask me. Over the months I came to recognize lots of familiar faces, learn most names, and eventually get to the point where I knew when most people arrived whether they were a member or visitor. Although a year into it, some would still get offended when I met them for the first time, as they let me know they were members. Only to later let me know that they hadn't been to church in nearly 9 months.

One very unfortunate scene I have seen more than I would like to admit, and I'm sure has played out on Sunday mornings throughout the world, would be the discrimination the local church has towards visitors. It's not done on purpose, and more times than not, it happens out of our own comfort level. Some mornings you would have a young family walking in, the husband in a nice button-down shirt, the wife with fixed hair, pretty dress, and the kids that were cute as well. They could hardly make it through the lobby while everyone made a B-line to make sure and greet the new couple. Conversations would end quickly as the new couple would be ushered in to a celebration. Maybe they knew someone there already, who really cared. Let's show them where the kid's ministry is, be sure and introduce them to the nursery director. Let's go in and make sure that other leaders in the church knew about the new couple and to catch them before or after the service. They were far from invisible.

Then the same morning it would be the couple walking in, clothes not as clean, perhaps the kids don't have the clean shoes. Dad is wearing a pair of worn out jeans, shirt unkempt, and not clean shaven. I see them walk in for the first time, nervous. They may get the token nod, and pointed them down the hall to the kid's department. Do we treat the first visiting family the same energy and enthusiasm as we treat the second visiting family? One is far from invisible, while the other is invisible before they even make it through the doors.

Lucky for me, I have a couple of sweet ladies that stand at the doors at our church and greet everyone that come in. Mrs. MaryAnn, Mrs. Connie, and Mrs. Mary Frances, will not let anyone enter into our sanctuary without learning everything about you. As my job has changed, and I no longer have the freedom to stand in the lobby and greet everyone. I rely heavily on Mrs. MaryAnn stopping me in the foyer to tell me anyone new that she saw come in, where they are sitting at, and that I need to go and introduce myself. I would venture to say that the foyer of every church in the world would benefit from having ladies such as these that love everyone that enters. They get it, and they know even by their weekly service, that their purpose each week is to welcome and make sure that no one enters our church invisibly.

I've been guilty of this very thing, unfortunately. I've seen people as they enter the church through my eyes with my heart. Rather than seeing them with God's eyes, we see them for how every other place sees them. We as a church see race, sexual orientation, social status, and past sins. Whether we want to admit it or not, we do see the world through our eyes rather than God's eyes. I can remember one Sunday morning running around the church making sure we had coffee in the class rooms, checking the thermostats, and all the random things that a pastor does in the morning to prepare for hundreds of people to enter into the church.

What is the goal of the church as we enter into the Sunday morning service? At what point is the church service a success? The number of people that come into the church? Perhaps we are successful when we have visitors? Did we make connections with other people? Did the worship team play the worship set amazingly? We as a church get sidetracked in our weekly rat race to have the ultimate service. We too often focus on the details, the PowerPoints, the lighting, the sound quality, the delivery of the message, and the numbers in attendance, rather than seeing people.

"I DON'T HAVE TIME FOR THAT"

The focus of our church service has become less about "We" and more about "Me." On one particular morning, I am making my rounds, and I look up as a gentleman walks into the church. I glance outside to see his beat-up car parked underneath the overhang. The worship team is wrapping up their practice, coffee is prepared, classes are full, service will be starting in less than half an hour, people are starting to show up for the service, and there is a guy in dirty clothes standing in my office distracting me from the day's work. We sat down and I remember thinking to myself: does he not know what day of the week it is. Turns out the man was passing through and needed a gas voucher. This happens regularly at the church. I remember filling out the voucher, giving it to him and then continuing with my morning. The gentleman was invisible to me, and it is painful for me to admit it. We get sidetracked, and make religion about

Me instead of We. When it is about Me, then everyone else is invisible.

That man needed a gas voucher that morning, which he received. He also needed someone to see him and pray for him. He needed to see that there was more to our church than just a gas voucher for his vehicle. People come through the doors every week that need more than a handshake, or a glance. The need to be seen. To not be ignored as people move from the center of the room to the outer room where it is more comfortable. We get distracted. We as a body should gather together to love one another, to encourage each other, and to build one another up. We get distracted though by everything that we want to see from the church rather than what God wants to see from us.

This incident at the time didn't speak much to me. To me, it was just a normal Sunday morning. I've handed out gas vouchers, hotel rooms, car batteries, etc, all on a Sunday morning. Sometimes before the service, during the service, or even after the service. It was a couple of months after this particular encounter that I felt the Lord speak to me in my quiet time. I felt like He highlighted this moment, and I was like, "God, he came in for a gas voucher, and I gave him exactly what he needed." The Lord highlighted, that I had been so caught up in making the service a complete success in my eyes, that I missed my true purpose, which was to be the gospel for this individual.

This moment of reflection broke my heart. I can remember praying that day and repenting for being so caught up in things that were not the main thing. The very next day someone walked into my office. It was the same man from 4 months earlier needing some assistance. I remember thinking to myself how exciting it was that God had allowed me this opportunity again. I met with the man, ended up praying with him, and for his family. I believe there was as much healing for me as there was for him.

If we want to be a church for the city and if we are going to fulfill the great commission, we have to ask the hard questions of what have we put on a pedestal in the church that is about "ME" and not about "WE"? Where are we missing opportunities to share the gospel, because we have become so focused on what our Sunday morning worship looks like, or our own hidden prejudices? Jesus never missed an opportunity to minister, whether it be a woman at the well, a man in a tree, a crippled beggar in the streets, or the woman who was untouchable. What opportunities do we miss, because we are so focused on what the next task at hand is, rather than taking the opportunity to be quiet, and pray, "God how do you want to speak to your people today?"

That simple prayer will impact your life, put you in more uncomfortable situations, then you could ever imagine. When we as a church move towards the "WE" mentality, then everything you do is for the Lord.

"TELL HIM HE IS A GREAT DAD"

There are endless opportunities to be a "light" in a "dark" world. When we quiet the distractions in our life long enough, it's surprising how often the Lord speaks to us, that we may not recognize it. The Lord doesn't speak to us only inside the four walls we call "church" today. It can be in your home, the grocery store, the mall, even in the local cell phone store. He is always speaking, we just have to decide if we are listening, and whether or not we want to respond.

I'll never forget, the time my mom needed a new phone. She had been staying with my grandfather in the hospital, who was very ill. It was the last time that I would get the opportunity to visit with my beloved Papaw in hospice care. I had spent the day with him, my mamaw, my aunt, and my mom. It was coming time for me to leave, and I really wasn't looking forward to that last hug, mainly because I knew it would probably be the last interaction, I would have with this man who had been such a father figure to me. He taught me so much and had been a father figure since the age of 9 when my dad walked away from me. He would even later serve as the best man in my wedding, a small token that I could offer him, that still was not adequate of everything he had meant to me.

My mother and I have always had a relationship, where I was the person she would come to with questions about anything. She was having cell phone issues and needed to go to the local cell phone store to get a new phone. My papaw was in hospice care, and they had rented a hotel room in this town, so that they could remain close to be with him. My mom was worried that her phone not working, could cause her to miss something important having to do with my papaw. If you know my mom, you know that as caring and compassionate as she is, the thought of buying a new anything is a terrifying experience. She asked me if I would go with her on the way out of town to buy her new phone.

I reluctantly went with my mom to the cell phone store. I thought perhaps it would be good to get out of the hospital, and have some down time away from all the sadness our family was experiencing. When we walked into the cellular store, I was immediately reminded why this experience could be so overwhelming. You have someone walk up with an IPAD, they take your info, and then you sit and wait on the next smooth-talking salesman to approach and try to sell you every single upgrade they have to offer.

The young man that waited on us was dressed nicely. He talked to my mom very politely and seemed like a nice guy. We went through the process and told him everything she didn't need, and what little she did. My mom needed to be able to text and play "Words with Friends" and that is all. Nothing more, nothing less. While we were in the store, I heard the familiar voice of the Holy Spirit, begin to speak to me about this young man. My first thought was "she just wants a new phone." I didn't come in here to share with anyone. Emotionally, I was spent. The whisper got louder, and then I was reminded it's not about you, it's about me telling this young man how I feel about him. So, I prayed, "Father, what would you want this man to know about himself today?" The Holy Spirit showed me a picture and it was this man, with a young boy who looked like he was 6-7 years old. They were very close, and happy in the picture I saw. Then the Holy Spirit said "tell him he is a great dad. Don't quit fighting, don't give up, that he will always be his father."

I remember sitting in this store, completely wrecked. All I wanted was a phone for my mom, and now I felt like the Lord was asking me to go out on a step of faith and share something completely out of left field with this stranger. I waited until the time was right, because he was at work and I needed to respect his workplace. I looked at him when he came over the final time, and was thanking us. I reached for his hand and shook it. I said "Hey, just so you know, I like to pray. I also believe that God still speaks to us, and I felt like the Lord wanted you to know something today." He nods, looking at me weirdly now, but listening. I continued, "I felt like the Lord showed me that you have a son, who is about 6-7, is this true?" He replied, "No, well, I did, but me and his mom just broke up." I continued and said, "Well the Lord, wanted me to tell you that you are a great dad. Don't quit fighting, don't give up, you will always be his father."

The salesman's eyes teared up, and he immediately began crying. Then he responded, "How'd you know that. That's crazy." He looked at my mom and asked her the same thing. She just laughed. I wasn't sure what was going on, but once he quit crying, he gave us the story. He and his girlfriend had been together for over five years, and he had been this boy's father, even though he had a different dad. They had recently broken up, and he was struggling because he wanted to maintain a relationship with the kid. His family had recently been telling him, that he wasn't even the boy's real father, and it was crazy for him to try and maintain a relationship with him, and even worse that he would try to support him financially. This man's family was telling him to walk away, cut ties, and move on.

God however was drawing him away from the window and telling him to keep fighting. That he is a good father, and that he would always be this child's father. Clearly this is a beautiful picture of what it looks like when our focus is on "WE" and not "ME." I just wanted a cellphone for my mom, but God wanted to affirm this man, his identity, and that he needs to fight for his son. This man, didn't have to walk into a church on Sunday to hear from God. He just needed to not be invisible, to be seen exactly where he was at, and someone to listen and step out in Faith.

A Church that is about "WE and Not ME," will begin to transform how we see not only our Sunday Services, but how we approach restaurants, cellphone stores, society, flights, schools, our workplaces. All these places are filled with individuals that are either in the window or have already fallen out. They all need to hear an on-time word, from an on-time Father, that loves them unconditionally, right where they are .

6 | THE FALL

"When he was sound asleep, he fell to the ground from the third story and was picked up dead." ACTS 20:9

I'm sure as the night wore on, Eutychus, had at some point felt the need to relocate in the room. Perhaps he was tired from a long day behind him. Regardless, there was something in the window that drew him there and causing him to lose focus on the task at hand. The window calls to us, offering a promise of fresh air, and lack of resistance. At the window he would have fresh air, and not have to deal with everyone else. This part of the room would look different. Often times, during service, I may have to get up and go to the balcony. The room looks so different when I am standing above and behind everyone. You can see who is taking notes, who is scrolling Facebook, what couple is sitting there awkwardly too close, the room looks different from this perspective.

My city looks different from outside the church as well. Going into laundromats with Dr. Travis, I hear a perspective on the church that you don't hear from inside the four walls. I hear single parent struggles and husbands looking for work. I hear about the foster care system in our communities that is so clearly broken. The church has identified the same issues that they want to combat, as the government, and the citizens. However, as long as the church is inward focused, and measuring success internally, then we will never succeed in carrying out the great commission.

The young man, did not realize that he was falling asleep. Often times in our own lives it is the consequence of our actions. For this young man, he chose to sit in the window, when he was tired, and losing focus. There was a certain force that drew him in, much like the merry-go-round that we discussed earlier. You are drawn to something until it is too late to realize that the outside of the building is way closer than you ever expected.

Sitting in the window has a consequence if you fall out. The fall was a process that the young man went through. We see it every day. Whether it be through friends in the church, who have been a part of our small groups, Sunday school class, or maybe in a new believer's class. Over time, they move to the outside of the room. Most of the time, it's a gradual move, until eventually they are no longer a part of the room, but have moved completely to the outer part of the room. Why do people find comfort in moving to the back of the room?

If you have ever stood on the edge of a room, or in the back of the service on a Sunday, what you see, is perhaps what Eutychus saw that evening. The backs of people's heads, no one's face, all intensely focused on what was happening in the front of the room. No one noticed what was tragically happening in the back of the room.

When we are all inward focused on what is only happening on the stage, or the front of the room, we miss everything happening behind us and around us. I know that this may seem like an odd concept to say that the people in the room were at fault, because they were doing exactly what they should do. They had come to a service, they were paying attention, they were worshipping, and they were in the word. However, I believe it is a great comparison, because when we become too focused on one aspect of the room, we lose perspective on who is around us.

"PERSPECTIVE COMES FROM YOUR SEAT IN THE ROOM"

One illustration that I love to use, is to set a can of Coke in the middle of the room on a table. Then set chairs up in a circle around the table, and ask everyone to describe exactly what they see. For most people a lot of the descriptions will have some similarities. All of the descriptions will include the color red, silver top, but then once we get past these two, some will describe a bar code, or lettering, maybe the ingredients. To one person sitting on the opposite side of the circle his description will be different from someone on the opposite side of the room. Does that mean that the other person is wrong? One description will say Coca-Cola, while another one will say the ingredients without the name on it. Which one is the correct description?

We all see things, from our own vantage point through our lens of perception. Those lenses will be shaped by everything. Past experiences, everything that we experience in life will have some sort of impact on our lens, or perspective for how we are seated in the room. It doesn't mean that it is wrong, because you are describing to me exactly what you are seeing. Often times in the church, we are so focused on making sure that everyone agrees with our description, that we lose focus and insight that not everyone is sitting in the same seat in which we are.

We get hyper focused on what we believe to be the correct perspective, and I believe that an outward focused church will be one, that stands up and moves around the room to take a view of everyone else's perspective. The key characteristics to the can are non-negotiable, it's color, what it contains, and the material in which it is made. The negotiables are what we perceive to be written on the can, based on our location in the room.

To get away from the "ME" mentality, I have to be more concerned with moving around the room, and seeing everything from God's perspective. If I am too focused on my perspective and what is happening right in front of me, then everyone else becomes invisible. 'John' at the laundromat, the flight attendant, and the salesman in the store. I no longer have time for these individuals, because I am only looking at things from my perspective. Everything outside of my box is now invisible.

Eutychus was invisible that night, not because he wasn't in the room. He was invisible, because no one was looking out for him, or saw him move out of the circle.

"CULTURAL EVANGELISM"

We have missed something important in our cultural evangelism. We have turned evangelism into a numbers game, or a mission trip. Let's travel to this location, make up T-shirts, share a program, paint a house, and convince you to say a prayer, then travel back. In a culture driven by numbers, so is the local church. Let's go out, and share the Gospel (which is awesome), but where is the developmental stage to evangelism? We have made it so easy to join the church, come visit, say a prayer, come to church, and congratulations you made it.

I would venture to say, that this was not what Jesus had in mind, when he commanded us to go out into all the world and share the gospel. Jesus told the disciples in Matthew 16 24, "If anyone would come after me, let him deny himself and take up his cross and follow me. For whoever would save his life <u>will lose it, but whoever loses his life for my sake will find it.</u>" This doesn't sound too enticing to me, to take up your cross, and follow me, deny yourself, lose your life.

The Gospel of Mark chapter 10 has the story of the rich young ruler.

"As He was setting out on a journey, a man ran up to Him and knelt before Him, and asked Him, "Good Teacher, what shall I do to inherit eternal life?" And Jesus said to him, "Why do you call Me good? No one is good except God alone. You know the commandments, 'DO NOT MURDER, DO NOT COMMIT ADULTERY, DO NOT STEAL, DO NOT BEAR FALSE WITNESS, Do not defraud, HONOR YOUR FATHER AND MOTHER.'"

And he said to Him, "Teacher, I have kept all these things from my youth up." Looking at him, Jesus felt a love for him and said to him, "One thing you lack: go and sell all you possess and give to the poor, and you will have treasure in heaven; and come, follow Me."

But at these words he was saddened, and he went away grieving, for he was one who owned much property. Mark 10:17-22

This young man, asks Jesus, how to inherit eternal life, and he has kept the commandments, Jesus felt Love for him, and replies that he must first give everything away, in order to receive eternal life. I don't believe that this verse was meant to say that Christians shouldn't have anything, or shouldn't seek possessions. I believe it was a heart issue for the young man, these possessions were things that the young man treasured. God is a jealous God, and he doesn't want just our obedience to the commandments. He wants everything, he wants our life.

I would venture to say that Jesus wouldn't have been very popular on the new membership team, at most churches today. Even when he called the disciples in the book of Matthew verse 18:

"As Jesus was walking beside the Sea of Galilee, he saw two brothers, Simon called Peter and his brother Andrew. They were casting a net into the lake, for they were fishermen. "Come, follow me," Jesus said, "and I will send you out to fish for people." At once they left their nets and followed him." Matthew 4:18-20

It says at once they left their nets and followed him. Peter was a fisherman, this was his livelihood, when he heard the voice of the Lord, and he left everything and followed immediately. He didn't try to work out some plan, he didn't go and try to sell his boat or nets. He went immediately.

The Lord is looking for followers that will drop everything immediately, lay down your life, and give it all to him. As you can see, the version of followers of Christ in the New Testament verses today's time, have changed drastically. We have altar calls, we pray with people, we baptize them, and we then are perplexed when we no longer see the young man, that we celebrated when he was baptized 6 months ago. How can a church baptize 5-10 people a year, yet 20 years later, still be the same size they were 20 years prior? We aren't challenging them to truly lay down their lives. The journey doesn't end as soon as you make the decision to follow Christ, it's only the beginning.

"INWARD SUCCESS VERSUS OUTWARD SUCCESS"

As long as the church is inward focused on inside successes such as: attendance, finances, baptisms, lighting, VBS, outreaches, and decisions for Christ, versus true outward successes, we will continue to have an outflow of invisible people moving from the inside of our culture and back out into the world.

Now there is nothing wrong with attendance. Healthy things will grow. Finances allow the churches to invest into outward ministries, missions, and our cities. Baptisms can show the growth of the congregation as it is an outward sign of an inward event. VBS when done right, can be an amazing outreach into our cities and communities. Please don't misunderstand this to say that I am against all the good things that the church does inside of the church.

Outward success, is in my opinion looking outward into our communities, and answering questions like: what can we do to lower the unemployment rate, how are we impacting the foster care system in our city, are we impacting the poverty culture in our city? It is possible to be successful with looking both inward and outward at ministry.

I'd venture to say it's the enemy that pre-occupied our concerns with the conditions of the room. I'm more concerned with the song choice of the worship team, whether or not the person doing the announcements mentions my ministry. Are the lights too dark or too bright? Rather than what are we as a church truly doing to impact our city with the Gospel of Jesus Christ. How are we walking with these new believers, to show them the steps along the way, of what it looks like to live a truly transformed life?

As a church, we have become inward focused, let's build the biggest programs and the best buildings. We will offer sport leagues, we will offer programming for our kids, let's try to bring as many people to our building as we can. We bring you in, then turn back towards the front of the room and focus on what is in the lights, yet fail to see the young man in the window. The new convert that is struggling financially, the mom that brought her kids to church, while her husband stayed home. Yet we continue to define our success by the number of people in our seats, as people fall out of the windows as quickly as they enter.

Jesus called his disciples to drop everything and follow him immediately. It cost everyone something. What does this look like in today's society? What are we doing to shift our focus as a church from everything internally, to externally impacting our city for the Gospel?

Our vision has to shift from the perspective we have taken in the circle, to moving throughout the room, and seeing everyone in that circle. We have to make the invisible people of our city visible. We have to see their problems, see their struggles, issues, children, finances, and we have to identify what are those situations and where are we called to serve, and not just ignore it.

7 | GET TO THE DOOR

"Paul went down and took him into his arms, and said 'don't worry he is alive'" Acts 20:10

I've always been curious what it looked like for the individual that actually saw Eutychus fall out of the window. You are sitting there, paying attention, focused on the meeting, and then all of a sudden from nowhere you hear a commotion, and perhaps they saw Eutychus feet as he exited the building. Did they see it? Was it silent? Was there a commotion? Then how do you get the attention of such a great speaker as Paul. Maybe it was Paul that witnessed the young man falling to his certain death.

Regardless, this had to be a very traumatic experience for the witnesses. We know it was traumatic for Eutychus. Can you imagine his thought process when he woke up to the falling sensation as he plummeted from a third story window? Did he wake up mid fall? Did he yell as he was falling? Perhaps he never did wake up, because it all happened so fast.

The natural reaction of the church gathering was probably to run to the window and look down at the young man laying broken in the street. I imagine a 30ft fall can do a lot of damage to an individual. What were the people saying? There was probably some discussion and commotion around the people that did not see the incident. I imagine, there were questions to how this exactly happened. One person would let another know, until everyone in the room was aware of the incident where the young man fell asleep in the window, and fell three stories to his death.

In a world of Social Media, where we are all instantly connected by the small "post" button on our smart phone or computer, we get a glimpse into someone's life immediately. In today's times, we learn of divorce, addiction, affairs, fights, disagreements, and arguments all in our newsfeed as soon as it happens. I can often times tell you how bad the school pick-up line or drop-off line was because someone is almost always going to post an update of how someone else honked at them, or cut them off. Recently my battery on my vehicle died, and my wife was having to drive out to where I was to give me a jump so I could go get it replaced. She jokingly made a post about it on social media, and before I could get to the store to replace it, I had two separate friends contact me asking if I needed help.

We live in what could be considered the most "connected" time that has ever existed. We follow everything our friends do from vacations to birthdays to even funerals. Social media allows you to peak into the lives of the famous. We feel like we know these individuals because we follow their daily and weekly activities. If you were to think about your close friends list on social media, you could probably give a pretty accurate indication of what their life is like. Although this account would solely be based on the perception that they want you to have.

When someone "falls out of the window" at our church or in our friend's circle, we then take the time to slow down enough to go back to their social media and we see all the signs. Today's Social Media is the Window that was in the Upper Room that night 2000 years ago. It happens far too often. We hear of someone falling out and we run to the window to look out. We look out and then we tell someone else what happened. We hear about a couple getting divorced and we go to their social media accounts. A young man dealing with addiction, and it's all over his social media page, or in his tweets.

More often than not, the signs have been there, in our news feeds, in our pews, in our cubicles at work, and yet these people have remained invisible to us. They only become visible when we hear their cries, see the destruction, or witness them falling out of the window.

"PAUL WENT DOWN"

However, Paul, doesn't run to the window. It says that he "went down and took him into his arms." Now this was in the middle of the night. Paul leaves the comfort of where he is at and he goes down the stairs into the streets.

Paul first had to recognize that something had happened. He didn't run to the window; he knew the last thing the kid needed was another person looking out of the window. He leaves the room, proceeding to go down from the third floor, to the ground floor, and then out into the streets where the young man lay dead.

Paul left the building and went into the street, and laid prostrate over the young man. Can you imagine, what it looked like? It could not have been a pretty site. This young man didn't just fall to the floor, he had fallen out of the window approximately 25 feet, landing in a way that would have killed him instantly.

This wouldn't have been a pretty sight Paul is walking up to. The people looked out of the window up above. Paul, however realized that this kid didn't need him looking out over him, he needed a miracle from God. He needed the presence of God over his life. The last thing Eutychus needed was a 4-point sermon from Paul about the dangers of sitting in a window and sleeping. Eutychus needed the presence, and Paul couldn't just stand in the doorway and throw it to him.

If we are going to be an outward focused church, then at some point our focus has to shift from not what can my church do for me, but what can I do for the Kingdom. At some point, in your life, you have to leave the window, leave the building, go out into the streets, and carry the presence of God into your City. The streets are full of men and women just like Eutychus. They had great intentions, but for some reason or another they became invisible, and they have fallen out of the window. It's going to be messy; you may have to leave the comfort of your office, and you may have to check your humility at the door. For Paul to lay over Eutychus, he would have had to lay prostrate from his knees, which would have been a dishonoring position, but he knew that this young man needed the presence of God, and he needed it right then.

Our world needs an encounter with the Presence of God. And you may be the only one who has that opportunity to share it with them. We have to love people exactly where they are at. Paul didn't try and carry him back upstairs so he could pray for him. I can't tell you how many times I have heard that people think the solution to their loved one's problems is getting them to church.

The Church isn't the solution. The presence of God is the solution. The gas voucher wasn't the solution that morning that the man came to the church. I treated it as such, he needed to be seen that morning, and I missed it. My office wasn't a safe place to come to, because I was only helping financially, but was failing to help spiritually. If Jesus died on the cross for everyone, then my heart should be for everyone to hear the Gospel. If I judge every group of people that doesn't look exactly like me, or maybe are struggling with their sins, then I am failing to love them. Jesus commanded us to Love our neighbors, not judge them.

Loving people groups that don't fit into your typical description of what the church looks like will be messy at times. But God can use anyone at any time to get his message across.

LUNCHROOM EVANGELISM"

I will never forget a young man that had started coming to our youth group. He was interested in a girl that was attending. She didn't want to be there either, but her father made her come each week. They would come each week, make jokes, and goof off. I often struggled because they didn't seem to be receiving anything. Each week I was disappointed, because I felt insufficient in my job as a youth pastor. I felt like I was failing to reach these two individuals.

One night we were out doing a treasure hunt and this young man went with me. Throughout the course of the night and through conversations you could really sense that the Lord was working on him. At the end of the night, I asked him if he would like to pray to receive Christ, and he said yes, so we prayed in the parking lot of the church. The next week I was on the high school campus eating lunch with students, and he invited me to come eat with him and his friends. I was excited! This kid that usually ignored me, now wanted to introduce me to his friends.

We were sitting there and I could tell a couple of the young men are being a little reserved. At one point, one of them let a bad word slip and he looked at me sheepishly and apologized. The young man that had invited me, looks across the table and says, "Dude, this is my youth pastor, don't talk like that!" I kind of laughed inside, as he proceeded to tell them how awesome our youth group was and how everyone needs to come with him to our service. One of the other students then asked him what church we went to. I'll never forget how he looked at me and said "What's the name of our church?" I gave him the name. He yells across the table the name of the church and says "it's awesome come with me." The young man responded that he went with his parents to their church; to which at my horror, the young man yells back across the table, "don't go there, they suck!" At this point, I'm trying to figure out how this conversation went so wrong, so quickly. While at the same time amazed at how this kid, who never wanted to go to church, had an encounter with the Lord, and now is evangelizing his table in the cafeteria. He didn't even know the name of the church, he just knew the encounter he had, and wanted all his friends to experience the same thing.

This young man, had access to students that I would never have access to. For some of those young men it may be their only encounter of the gospel. Granted it wasn't polished, and we shouldn't go around telling other kids that their church "sucks." However, the intensity was right though, and the heart was right too. This kid couldn't even tell you what the word evangelism meant, but he was living it. He would later be baptized, along with his sister and her boyfriend, all whom he had a key role in introducing to the Lord.

51

If I learned anything from this encounter, it's that, people need to be seen, exactly where they are. I would have never met any of these kids had I just stayed in the church. When you leave the walls of the church and enter into the streets, you begin to see all the ways in which God will use his people to get his Gospel outside. This kid, newly baptized, shared the Gospel more in that lunchroom, then I would say most of the congregants in our church do in a lifetime. These kids didn't need the youth pastor to sit there and correct them for their language, or lifestyle. They needed their friend to say, this is what's happened in my life, and you really need this in yours.

"WHICH ONE WILL YOU BE?"

My challenge today is which person are you going to be? Are you content with simply walking to the window with everyone else to witness the destruction that happens when someone falls or has fallen? When we stand in the window, we don't have to leave our safe confines of the building. It's much easier to stand in the window.

Are you going to choose to be like Paul, and leave the comfortable confines of your church, and go out into the streets, to carry the Presence of God into the World? It won't be easy. There will be messes that you encounter. Your heart will break for a society that has always existed, but you never noticed, simply because you've never asked God to allow you to view society through his lens. It may be uncomfortable, when you pray for the person in the line at the grocery store, but everything will change when you walk outside your comfortable walls and view the world with the eyes of the father.

8 | GO WITH THEM

"They went back upstairs and ate the Lord's Supper" Acts 20:11

The street would have been dark while a young man laid in the streets with the visible signs of destruction to his body. Perhaps there was blood and dirt on his clothes as he lay there lifeless in the middle of the street having just fallen to his sudden and unexpected death. I'm sure there was commotion above in the window, as the people who had just been with him upstairs, viewed from their safe place up above.

Paul's dark figure emerges from the doorway down below, and he probably had to lift his robe to his knees, to lay down over the man. There was no hesitation in any of his actions. He begins to pray for the young man and cover him in his prayers when all of a sudden, through the gift of miracles, life comes back into this young man who seconds earlier lay lifeless. But Paul doesn't stand in the street and celebrate. He simply takes the young man back upstairs where they share the Lord's Supper.

It would have been easy for Paul to sit the young man down and lecture him about how dangerous it is to sleep in the window. Eutychus, by this point in time probably was overly aware of the dangers associated with sleeping in the window. Paul however, took the young man back upstairs and shared communion with him.

53

"I KNOW WHO YOU ARE"

We all have experiences and we know someone who had failed sometime in their life. We have a strong memory when it comes to those close to us. One of the forces that draws people away from the church in the first place and then later prevents them from returning is the exponential force of shame and un-forgiveness. The last thing they really need is for us to remind them of their shortcomings. The devil reminds them of that daily.

More time's then not, when I've seen prodigal's return to the church, there is an alarming number of people in the congregation that say "well, we shall see if it sticks this time" or "we all know that they struggled with this, I hope they overcome it this time." Paul doesn't do that with Eutychus though. He simply takes him back into the upper room and shares the Lord's Supper with him.

I mentioned my father and his battle with alcoholism. He left my mom and our family when I was nine years old. We continued through life and things were very estranged. We would see him on holidays and talk to him on the phone every so often. I developed a safe guard with him as a young man. I would never expect anything from him, so that I wouldn't be disappointed as I had so many times growing up. Dad continued to drink. He owned a construction company, and would eventually move himself and the crew to Florida where he could work on continuous projects in the Orlando area.

By the time I was thirty years old I had three children and I was happily married to my college sweetheart. We were living in Louisiana, involved in an amazing church. I was in financial sales, and life was great. The last year we lived in Louisiana my father's alcoholism had escalated to a point where he was not doing so well, physically or spiritually. He would end up giving his business away and moving to Louisiana to live closer to me. I remember that first year. I stayed so frustrated, as I felt like the solution to getting my father out of his problems was to get him to church.

I would invite him continuously to the church every single time the doors were open, but he never had any interest. He was content being in the same town with me and his grandkids, but that was the extent of our relationship. My wife and I had accepted a new position back in my hometown in Arkansas, so we were preparing to move our family from Louisiana. We had decided to buy a house in Arkansas and fix it up while we waited on our house in Louisiana to sale. I would travel to Arkansas on Monday mornings, work all week at the bank, renovate the house in evenings, and then traveling back to the family on Fridays after work. My father, who was skilled in carpentry lived with me in Arkansas while we renovated the house. I can remember coming home from work, and he and his large pit bull would still be sitting in the living room, having done nothing while I was away at work all day. It was frustrating to me, but we would get to work, and work on the house into the late hours of the evenings.

This routine went on for about 4 months, and my father and I grew closer as the months and projects progressed in the renovation. Of course, he had no income, or vehicle and relied on me to financially support him. It was the first time in my life that I was able to have conversations with my dad about heavenly things. He re-lived some of the old days of evangelism. I could always see the twinkle in his eyes as he would reminisce about the old days of hitchhiking from town to town and sharing the gospel.

I started to see my father for who he was as a person. He became less and less invisible to me. The alcoholism was still there, but it was manageable to say the least. I could always smell it, but it wasn't to some of the extremes that I have witnessed with others. Once I got past the smell of cheap whiskey, long unkempt hair, worn out jeans and boots, I could see a man, who at one time had so much promise. I could see a man who still had a love for the Lord. He still prayed every day throughout the day. Perhaps his inner struggles were just that, inner issues and struggles that he never could fully deal with.

My father went on to live three more years before his body just could not keep up any more. Those last three years of his are ones that I will always treasure. As I said earlier, he was no longer invisible. We would have our issues, but eventually he started coming to church with me and the family. My father would show up to church with a truckload of people he had met that day. Even as a 57-year-old alcoholic with nothing, he still was one of the most effective people I knew when it came time to invite someone to church. I'm embarrassed to say this, but I often times struggled with this image. I struggled with the fact that my father was coming to church with the stench of cheap whiskey on his breath, and would share the gospel with other people. It was embarrassing to have him sit next to me with his 3 or 4 friends that he had brought to church. That last two years of his life he was with us nearly every Sunday and honestly there wasn't one of those days that I was happy and not embarrassed to sit with him.

One of the last spiritual conversations my father and I shared was about two weeks before his death. We were building a deck on the back of our house, when he mentioned something about God. I looked straight at him and asked if he ever still talked to God? He said, "Son I speak to him every day." I then decided to take it a step further, and asked what God actually said to him when he heard his voice? He then opened up and talked about all his past failures, but that God still loved him. He knew that what he was carrying spiritually had passed, his time had passed, but that God had promised him that it had moved to his son. That he was praying I would carry on his heart for evangelism and the gospel.

My father would suffer a stroke two weeks later, and I can remember sitting with him in the hospital. He was unable to communicate, just mumbling and pointing to things. We were in the hospital for almost a week, as time wore on, his body was going through the obvious withdrawals from his alcoholism. That Thursday, they came in to take him to have a CT scan, wanting to monitor his brain to see if the damage had spread. I leaned over, kissed him on the cheek, and told him I loved him. To which in a clear voice, I heard the only words I had heard from him all week, "I love you too, son." Dad would suffer a second stroke while in the CT Scanner, and he went to be with the Lord two days later.

"THE OFFENDED SON"

While my father was no longer invisible to me, along with that, came all my pre-conceived judgements over the man and his struggles. It would be years later when I was preparing a message for the church about the popular passage of the Prodigal Son. I wanted the focus to be on the son, who was returning home, similar to Eutychus, after he had fallen through the window.

Although, I had been on staff at the church for eighteen months, this would be my first opportunity to speak to the congregation. Having the opportunity to preach on the "Prodigal Son" seemed fitting, I had been born into this church, baptized at the age of seven, then moved off for 25 years before returning. I always viewed myself as the prodigal son of my local church in some sort of way.

This story, most of the time when it is told, the focus is on the son, and the pretense is we all can return home and be welcomed by our Father. When the prodigal is not the focus, then the story or sermon may shift to the Father, and how instantly he welcomed him back. A beautiful picture of the Father running down the path to meet his son, before anyone could get back to him.

That week, as I prepared my message, I was in the sanctuary practicing. This would be my first time to speak to the congregation. I was excited, nervous, and all the other emotions that come with it. I was reminded of that last spiritual conversation with my father, and I thought to myself, how proud my dad would be if he could be present to hear my message. Then I looked to the seat in the front and I pictured him sitting there, in his old cowboy boots, and worn out leather coat. These were the only things I had kept when I had cleaned out his stuff 3 years prior. As I sat there on the stage, I felt like the Lord spoke to me, and said, "He was the prodigal, he did come back, and I welcomed him back."

Then I realized, where I fit into this whole story. I was the offended brother. I had been praying for years for my dad to come back to the Lord. It had been happening over the course of the three years we spent together before he passed, but I missed it. I had missed it, because I was too caught up in all of his sin to recognize the beauty of his return. I was the offended son. I was too caught up in the stench of his alcoholism, and here he was sharing the gospel with different people every week and carrying them to church. And I was too worried that someone would notice that this man smelled like cheap whiskey. I couldn't celebrate in the feast. I missed it, because I was too busy pointing out all of his issues. I was the offended son.

That Sunday morning, I would preach the message for the congregation, wearing those worn out cowboy boots of my father. I also brought a coat rack on stage, and hung his old leather coat on it. I shared with the congregation the passage, not the prodigal son, but I shared about the Offended Son. I felt my father was right there next to me, the entire time.

"COME GO WITH ME"

So often in our life, as we deal with people who like Eutychus or my father have fallen out of the window, we have a decision to make. This decision comes not long after there is new life. Are we going to be like Paul? Are we going to carry the young man back into the service to share in communion? Are we going to be like the offended son, and miss the celebration?

To miss the celebration, that is the easiest of the choices. It's easy to see everything that is wrong with someone, and move on in our relationships. Their life has consequences. Everything we do has consequences. As a church, it's easier when someone falls away, to let them move on. For some reason we don't want people in the church to know that we deal with all kinds of issues. We sweep topics like: Pornography, debt, divorce, mental illness, and addictions all under the rug. We can't let the public know that this is happening in our congregation. Those types of issues don't happen in a healthy church. They only happen on the dark streets like the one that the young man had fallen into before Paul carried him back in.

We see it in our communities, but we don't want to invite that into our congregations. It's so much easier to pray for the individual and then move on. It's easier to just give them a helping hand and move about our day to the next task, like I had done with the man I mentioned earlier who showed up to our church on a Sunday morning before service. Or, we can choose to be like Paul. That's not the easier of the two, and it's going to involve walking with them. It's going to involve meeting with them, discipling them, and having tough conversations. This young man needed Paul to help him back upstairs. There was a journey and process and whatever it was, Paul was there for it. To be successful with this we have to be able to see the person, see the heart of the person, and love them with God's heart.

We celebrate as a church, when someone comes back into the kingdom; when a prodigal son returns. Yet we miss the actual celebration.

If we aren't carrying the broken, the addicted, or the spiritually dead, back upstairs into the upper room, then how effectively are we actually being in carrying the Gospel to the world? At this point we are carrying an experience, but not a lifestyle impact. I believe the outcome of Eutychus would have been different if Paul had simply prayed for him, congratulated him on being alive, and sent him on his way.

If we are going to be a church for our City, then we have to figure out a way to move from the Salvation experience in the street, and walk with them upstairs with them into the upper room. We have to quit treating Evangelism with the approach that the decision they make and the prayer is the end result, when it is actually only the beginning.

If you notice, the verse continues with Paul continuing preaching throughout the night. I believe this speaks to the thought that the Salvation experience doesn't culminate when the prodigal returns inside. The story didn't end with Eutychus return. We have to find an effective way to disciple, minister, and walk with individuals, to truly live life together.

9 | LAY DOWN YOUR TITLE, PICK UP YOUR TOWEL

"So he got up from the meal, took off his outer clothing, and wrapped a towel around his waist" John 13:4

Time with my dad was always important, but that meant summer's and holidays on his construction site. After the divorce we would see him on holidays and maybe for a week or two in the summer. Of course, he couldn't afford to take off work, so that meant that I usually was on the construction site. I doubt my contribution was that great, but I always loved getting to carry a tool belt and do whatever odd job my dad had for me, whether it be collecting scraps, cleaning up the site, or cutting door frames out. Eventually as I got older the jobs would get more detailed and my contribution was greater. My father, wasn't always the best person to teach me things, but there was one lesson he taught me that I have always valued. He used to say "never ask anyone on your team to do something that you wouldn't do yourself." This meant to me, that there was nothing on the jobsite too little that my dad wouldn't do. No job was ever below him, and I respected that.

Today in ministry, it's easy for us to become so focused on what's happening in the box that we call "Church" that we miss what's happening outside the four walls. Church isn't something that we schedule for once or twice a week. We look at different ministry opportunities and treat some of them as they are below us, that job isn't for me, or it isn't the best fit. In a consumerism church, we hesitate to step into volunteer roles, because we would rather not have to work in the nursery this week. I

61

don't want to serve on the worship team, because then I have to give up one night of the week for practice. Of course, the church is full of individuals that serve every single week, but by and large, the typical sanctuary is filled with individuals that believe that the Church is just there to serve them once a week for an hour or two.

When we transform to a church for the city, when we are like Paul and leave the comforts of the building and move into the streets, then we recognize that we are carrying the presence of God wherever we go, and nothing is below us, because Jesus modeled it best.

"WHO IS THE GREATEST"

On the night of the last supper, Jesus had sent the disciples to prepare the borrowed room, for what would be one of the most well-known moments in biblical times, The Last Supper. Imagine the weight of the moment spiritually as Jesus walked into the room. The disciples are arguing over which of them is the greatest.

There would be a wash basin between the door that they entered and the table at which they would share the Passover Feast. Jewish Customs are that the lowest of the lows would be the one to wash everyone's feet. It was law at this time. It was against the law for even a Jewish slave to wash someone else's feet, if there was a Gentile Servant available.

When the disciples walked in, they knew someone would have to do it, but no one wanted to, because they were jockeying for position. Jesus walks over, takes off his outer garment, and picks up his towel and ties it around his waist. In an instant he went from Master and Teacher, to Servant.

The disciples were all shocked as they witnessed this. The disciples were no stranger to this custom. They were adults and had been in this custom for their whole lives. This was a feast that they shared every year. Peter, was the first one to comment, "Lord don't wash my feet," but it was the purpose of Jesus to become the servant in this moment.

In Exodus 30: 17-21 it is written, "Then the LORD said to Moses, Make a bronze basin, with its bronze stand, for washing. Place it between the tent of meeting and the altar, and put water in it. 1Aaron and his sons are to wash their hands and feet with water from it. 2Whenever they enter the tent of meeting; they shall wash with water so that they will not die. Also, when they approach the altar to minister by presenting a food offering to the LORD, they shall wash their hands and feet so that they will not die. This is to be a lasting ordinance for Aaron and his descendants for the generations to come."

These were the instructions God gave to Moses for the Temple, he instructed that their Hands and Feet should be washed, in order that they do not defile the Temple. This was a requirement. The people in the room could not partake of the Passover, unless they had first obeyed the laws. Jesus took the place of the Servant, and prepared the men, so they would be able to approach the Table and Covenant. Jesus knew this as he approached the water basin.

He laid down his title, and picked up his towel, so that we can all approach the banquet table. We have to do this as well. We have to become servants to our cities, our neighborhood's, and our workplaces. If we don't pick up our towel, and lay down our title, what opportunity will be missed because someone wasn't prepared to approach the banqueting table?

Jesus wasn't asking anyone to do anything that he didn't do first. He calls us to Love.

"Very truly I tell you, no servant is greater than his master, nor is a messenger greater than the one who sent him.17Now that you know these things, you will be blessed if you do them." John 13:16-17

We have to turn from the traditional approach of church where we are all focused on the front of the room, and the one speaking, to getting outside the four walls to figure out what we can do to impact our city for the Kingdom. We won't be able to do this, unless we lay down our Title, and pick up our towel.

The people we encounter in the grocery stores, on the streets, in the laundromats, the flight attendants, and the cell phone salesman, every one of them, are needing an encounter with the Lord. It may never happen if our mentality is simply that it is someone else's job to share the Gospel with them. The young man at the cafeteria table had no idea of the name of his church, but he did know that he wanted his friends to experience the transformation that he had experienced. None of those transformations happen, unless we as a church, can lay down our title and pick up our towels. Jesus called us to be servants. He called us to love the world.

We confuse that with thinking he called us to have amazing church services, large attendance and big offerings. How many people do we encounter in a day, that are simply needing a word from God, and we have access to exactly this? We are open vessels to him, we hear his voice, yet it doesn't fit into our day. Until we lay down our title, and pick up our towels, we will be unable to effectively impact our city, schools, and workplace.

It can happen anywhere In Psalms 24:1 NIV: **"The earth is the LORD's, and everything in it, the world, and all who live in it."** We are in that relationship with God, and we owe it to the people we encounter daily to share it with them. Notice it doesn't involve standing on a street corner, holding up a sign that condemns everything that they are doing wrong. When we are carrying the presence of God, we are also in turn carrying his attributes, you will have a heart to love everyone.

It may be as simple as volunteering at the schools, serving in your church nursery, opening the doors and greeting people. There are many ways that we can lay down our titles and pick up our towels. A title is nothing more than a description of a position that we have reached. We all carry the same title, and that is a son or daughter of the king. We are to copy Jesus who was the ultimate servant.

10 | A SHEPHERD WITH NO SHEEP

"The LORD is my shepherd, I lack nothing." Psalms 23:1

I can remember feeling at a very young age, that I was called into ministry. Different people had spoken it over my life that I would be a pastor. My parents and other parental figures had always encouraged me in this. I can remember being confused when I had graduated from college. I knew that eventually I was going to be in ministry, but I didn't know how that was or what it would look like.

I remember a very valuable conversation with my mentor, Wayne Drain, who was there all those years ago when my father had left us and the church. I have a picture of Wayne in my office, and it is from my baptism at the age of seven years old. In the picture, I am coming out of the water, my father is holding me in his arms, and right beside him is his dear friend Wayne.

Wayne made a promise to me the day when the church showed up to pack our house up. It was he and I, along with my beloved Papaw. In the back of the U-Haul, Wayne looked down at me and promised that he would always be there for me, and if ever I needed anything that he would be there to walk me through it. It was 26 years later, when I finally made a decision to enter into full time ministry that I would call Wayne up to seek his wisdom and would end up moving my family to Russellville to serve in his church.

Over the years, Wayne has always made time for me, and hanging out with him was like being in the security of a father figure. He performed my wedding for my wife Stacy and I, but it was a conversation not long after I graduated college that made a lasting impact on me and my life. I said to him, "Wayne, I know that God has called me into the ministry and to the church, but I don't know what I should do about that." He asked me, "Do you feel like God is telling you to go to a specific church?" I replied that I didn't feel called to anything specifically. I was graduating college, coming out of a tremendous college ministry, and already had a job secured as an investment representative. He said, "well you know that you are called to eventually be a pastor, so don't wait for that day. Pastor everything you are involved in, serve everywhere you can serve, and learn everything you can from where you are at." He was basically telling me to live in the moment, and do everything I could to the best of my ability.

It would be 14 more years before I actually "entered" into a ministry position. However, it was everything that happened inside of those years that would actually prepare me for my calling. It was the breakfast clubs with high school students, it was serving on the Missions board, financial stewardship teams, volunteering with the youth ministry, serving in any shape or capacity that needed my attention.

"BE PRESENT WHERE YOU ARE"

People all the time tell me, how they wish they worked in ministry so that they could do "the Lord's work". I guess in their mind, somewhere it says in scripture that in order to serve in ministry, you have to draw a paycheck from the church. Wayne's wisdom to me, was be present and pastor where you are at. Be faithful with that which is right in front of you. It is written in Luke 16: 10: "Whoever can be trusted with very little can also be trusted with much, and whoever is dishonest with very little will also be dishonest with much"

How could I ever be a pastor or a leader to a large group of people, if I wasn't effectively discipling the people that had been placed in my immediate circle of influence? Our church in Russellville didn't start in a building full of people. It started 48 years ago, in the upper room of a building on a college campus with only a few college students.

I still laugh, at my approach to entering into full time ministry. I spent years in the financial world, and somehow was just waiting on a postcard to come in the mail from God with my assignment. Well that never happened, but thanks to the advice of my mentor years before, I was diligent in my relationships and discipled and served those around me when I had the opportunity.

We are all called into ministry, I tell my kids that they have access to individuals that I would never have access to in ministry. One of my younger sisters is a kindergarten teacher, and she has access to those children every day, and their parents. I see how she loves them, gives them a safe environment, prays for them and their families. She is in ministry, and that is her ministry. It isn't happening inside the four walls of a structure that we have defined as the church. She is the church, and is carrying the presence of the Lord into her environment every day.

"SHEPHERDS EXIST FOR THE SHEEP"

Shepherds are one of the key references to Jesus in scripture. We are his flock; he is the Shepherd. A shepherd cares for the flock, and takes care of it. The Good Shepherd protects his flock from the enemy. He is the ultimate Servant. The Shepherd exists for the Sheep; the Sheep don't exist for the Shepherd.

The Shepherd is one of the ultimate examples of Servanthood. *John 13:16-17 "Very truly I tell you, no servant is greater than his master, nor is a messenger greater than the one who sent him. Now that you know these things, you will be blessed if you do them.*

If we are going to be immersed in Jesus, and take on his qualities, if we are going to lay down our title and pick up our towel and become a Servant, then we have to be on the lookout for who to serve. Who is 'our Flock' that we are called to? It's our homes, schools, workplaces, and neighborhoods. All of these are individuals that have been entrusted to us to minister to, that we must be good stewards over our relationships with. People in vocational ministry are not the only Shepherds.

Often times I have people come to the office to let me know that they feel called to ministry. We have discussions and talk about what they may be doing, or what they could be doing to prepare, if this is truly the direction God is calling them to serve in. I will always ask one question during the meeting, "Tell me about who you are serving now?" It opens the door for great conversations, because if we can't be diligent with the 1 or 2 that God has already given us, why would he give us 10-20 or a church of thousands? A shepherd with no sheep, is just some man walking in the wilderness.

He/She may have all the tools required to be a shepherd, a staff to guide the sheep, a weapon to protect them from harm, the right clothes to be protected from the elements, and the necessary tools and equipment to live out in the fields. But without the sheep, you are merely surviving on the land. You have to lay down your title, pick up your towel, and figure out where you can best serve. Who has been placed in your path for you to disciple?

I admire our Children's Pastor at our church so much for this characteristic. He and his wife have been our Children's pastor for about 6 years, but his position is a part-time position, so he has employment outside the church. Anthony feels called to minister to children of this age, so his job is as a Physical Education teacher at a local elementary school. His impact and reach are far greater on this campus then at the church, and the reach of his ministry is phenomenal. We see time and time again people from the community attending his events at the church, because they love interacting with Coach Ross in the schools. He is a shepherd, and a great steward over his flock.

We have been blessed with this time and time again at our local church, where I see people not only serving in one capacity in our local church, but they are doing it out in the community.

A Shepherd With No Sheep

I can remember the conversation with our Senior Leader Chris, when he was transitioning into the role of serving as our Senior Leader. Wayne, whom I had mentioned earlier had been the Senior Founding Pastor for 45 years. Chris was one of our Elders in the church. He is a successful businessman with an amazingly generous heart. It has been his vision for our City that has had so much impact on my heart personally for truly being a church for the City.

He and I had countless discussions in the year of transition within our church. We definitely did not have all the answers for what the transition would look like. For Chris, it was trying to figure out what it would look like, stepping into the forefront of an existing church, that would put him in the key place to cast the vision for our local church, that he felt like the Lord was speaking to him. For me, it was transitioning from having a Senior Pastor, that was at the church every day and interacting in the day to day functions of the local church.

My role transitioned as well with Chris coming on board. My role in ministry would now be to carry out the mission and vision that was cast by Chris and the Elders of our local church. I learned how to work closely with a Senior Leader, and figure out what he needed to know on a weekly basis at the church, and what he was giving me the authority to carry out on my own, without having to bother him with the details.

One day early into the conversation, I remember making a statement to him, and in the statement, I mentioned that he was bi-vocational. He quickly came back, with a correction. It wasn't in a corrective manner where I felt like I had messed up. However, he was very clear, that the term Bi-vocational carried the weight that he had two jobs that were not the same. It carried the context that during the week, when he was at this location, he would be a business person, while other parts of the week, he would be the Pastor. When in fact, he was called to pastor the city, and this wasn't something that just happened inside the four walls of a structure we called the church.

This was the most declarative statement I have heard from anyone on truly being a Church for the City. All of us were called into ministry, and all of us are carrying something that is meant to impact and change our culture for the kingdom. I share this to encourage you today, that where ever you may be in your journey, you don't have to wait. When Jesus came into your heart, you were fully immersed into the Kingdom.

It's your decision with how this immersion will impact you and your life. Will you choose to be one of the ones in the upper room that failed to see the young man making his way to the window and eventually falling out into the midnight air? Will you be like Paul, and be the kind of immersed believer, that recognizes the authority that you carry, to actually leave the building and go out into your city and streets to make a lasting impact on your environment?

11 | WE OWE IT TO THE WORLD

This journey has been a brief glimpse into a passage that realistically only covers a brief encounter in the New Testament book of Acts. We don't know much about the young man Eutychus, or what happened to him later in life on his spiritual walk.

What we do know, is like far too many other people after him, he set out on one path, only to tragically end up in a situation that wasn't what he originally planned on happening. There were other people in that room, and in a far too familiar event, they were all present when the invisible man fell out of the window.

As a body of believers, many times we have witnessed someone walking away from a relationship with the Lord, and it has become increasingly all too common for us to move on and not be impacted to the actual consequences of what happens when someone "falls out of the window." We have become numb to the reality, that this person is no longer walking with the Lord. We have chosen as a society to simply move on with the routines of our daily life, meanwhile the invisibles are filling up our streets, our workplaces, our schools, all fallen from the window, with no real hope of ever returning.

I could preach a thousand sermons, and never have the encounters that I have had when I simply stepped out of the comforts of my environment, my building, and chose to walk in the streets with the authority that has been given to me. I could stand down front at the alter every Sunday for 10 years, and would never have the encounters that I have been blessed to have with people like 'John' in the laundromat, or the lady in the grocery store, or the cellphone salesman.

The one thing they all have in common, is they are not found inside the four walls of our structure that we have come to know as the modern-day church. The church in Acts was not meant to exist inside the confines of a building once a week. It existed in homes, in the marketplaces, and on the streets. We have gotten comfortable as a society with the separation of our church structures and the world. We have given our hospitals, our education, the orphans, the homeless, and the broken people in society away. It's easier if we don't encounter them inside the church. It's easier to not have to engage in conversations with how we are to impact these individuals.

When you make a commitment to follow Christ, it comes with instructions. The Bible and our relationship with God are no longer a long list of "Do's" and "Don't's." It's more of a love letter from God, throughout the passages. Inside this love letter include some key commands or instructions. The instruction to love your neighbor, notice we aren't commanded to judge our neighbor, but to love them and to see them exactly where they are at. We are wise to follow Paul's example with the young man, as he didn't stop his relationship once the boy had been brought back to life. He carried him back into the safe place, back into the relationship, and he shared communion with him.

To live as Paul did and to fully reach our society with the gospel, we will have to lay down our title and pick up our towels so that we can fully grasp what it means to be a servant. Leaders aren't simply leaders because of their titles. They are leaders when they take on a true servant's heart. When we begin to see the world through the father's heart and his lens, we will see all the pain and suffering that is surrounding us. It will begin to break our hearts for the lost, and we will live each day with the intensity that Paul had as he flew down from the third floor and into the streets to pray for the young man. That is the intensity that I want and I continue to pursue in my daily walk with the Lord. That is the intensity that I pray has entered into your heart as you read through these pages.

In the end, we have all been in the upper room. Some of us have been in the middle of it, and sadly many of us may have been the young man drawn to the window. We all have had that encounter. We are called now to carry that encounter out into the world. We owe it to the world. We owe it to ourselves.

The upper room is a great place to be. We are told by the writer of Hebrews in chapter 10 and verses 24-25: "And let us consider how we may spur one another on toward love and good deeds, not giving up meeting together, as some are in the habit of doing, but encouraging one another—and all the more as you see the Day approaching." We are called to look outward into our cities, while continuing to look inward and encourage one another, as we live in covenant with one another.

My father and Wayne when I was baptized in 1987.

Wayne and me, at my licensing service in 2015.

My Father and Warnock at a football game not long after he came to live with us. 2008

Steve (Pop) adopted me and raised me as his own son. I got to surprise him ringing the bell after his last radiation treatment. 2019

Epilogue

This book, has been on my heart, for several years now. The first time that I preached this message was Palm Sunday, 2015. I felt like the Lord spoke to me at that time, through prayer that this was a message that needed to be communicated. The seed was planted, but in true fashion, I would work on it sparingly over the next four years. In January 2019, while attending a worship and prayer event, I felt like the Lord spoke to me again. I journaled it down:

"Like a tide coming in the night, I am coming for my city. When I come it will be a mighty flow that will engulf everything in its path. Washing the impurities from the shores it will also bring a shift to structures that have long been in place but have failed to continue its purpose. When my tide recedes, there will be new structures, new foundations, new walls. New streets, that will lead the lost to me. New Day. All things will be new.

Nothing will be able to contain nor restrict the flow of my water. Do not fear, for we shouldn't fear that which is good. My tide will fill every school until it flows through the rooftops. My name will be glorified through the schools. Government structures will be overflown with my glory.

It's time to run towards the water, rather than running from it. All things new. Do not Fear.   This water will be filled with Love, not Judgement. Peace not turmoil. Abundance not poverty, Joy not sadness. All things new." January 25, 2019

In November of 2019, I was challenged by a question. "What are things that the Lord has spoken to you and asked you to do, but you have not achieved?" Writing a book on the church leaving the building and going into the streets was #1 on that list. Then the next question was: What are you doing each day to achieve those tasks that the Lord has spoken to you? I felt convicted, I knew what this book would say, I had written it several times over the 4 years in my head. Although I never took the time to sit down and actually write it because I was too busy with life each day.

I am not a writer, it has never been my strong suit. Perhaps, the Lord asked me to write it, because He knew it would be impossible without Him. Once "The Man in the Window" - Creating a Culture of Evangelism in a Modern-Day World was finished, an odd thing happened. The COVID-19 Pandemic. I was travelling in the UK in March of this year for a church conference, and we would end up coming home a day early, as the pandemic spread throughout the world. The following week, churches all across the nation would be forced to systematically shut their doors. The world as we knew it was in a shift. Sporting events, schools, restaurants, the entertainment industry and even churches were overnight forced out of the "building" and into the streets.

The new streets today are mostly relatable to the Internet, social media, websites, etc. I would liken the internet to the Roman roads some 2000 years ago, that the early church used to travel and spread the gospel to all the lost. The Romans did not have that in mind, but God can use anything for his greater purpose.

Church leaders are currently being forced to come up with creative ways to get beyond their buildings. I've been encouraged by all the media content that has been produced in this new day. It feels like a Sabbath for the Church. People are spending more time with family. And taking walks each day. Family Zoom calls are a daily thing.

It will be interesting to see how the church responds to this. I believe that tomorrow will never look like yesterday again. My hope in this time is that the church will continue to find new and creative ways to continue to move outside the building and into the streets using creative ways to carry the Gospel forward. Unlike COVID-19, the Gospel does not have an expiration date. It is a timeless message. It is our challenge as believers to take it and run our race.

Be Encouraged.

David J. Howell

Also available @ Amazon:

"The Man in the Window" Workbook

A six week guide, designed to lead you and your team on a journey. Carrying the gospel from the building and four walls and out into the streets.

For more info: www.davidjhowell.com